DROPSHIPPING

DROP SHIPPING: A STEP-BY-STEP GUIDE FOR BEGINNERS TO BUILD A PASSIVE INCOME STREAM USING THE DROP SHIPPING BUSINESS MODEL FOCUSED ON E-COMMERCE MARKETING (SHOPIFY, AMAZON FBA, EBAY).

Table of Contents

Description

Dropshipping has revolutionized the way we do business online. While it might sound intimidating to beginners, the fundamentals could not be simpler. The traditional methods of ecommerce are usually what we think of when selling items online. You advertise and market the item, buyers pay and leave their postal address, you package and send the item. While this might be great if you have all the time in the world to package and handle items, in today's fast paced world there has got to be an easier way.

This is where dropshipping takes the stage as the cornerstone of online business. The idea is simple yet unique. You advertise your item and buyers pay and leave their postal address, only this time instead of hassling with a warehouse of items to pack and send you simply leave the details of the items and the buyer's address with your designated drop shipper. The drop-shipper, from their much larger warehouse, then packs and sends the item on your behalf.

The beauty of this system is that you literally have the ability to make money without prior investment. Having no inventory to weigh you down is an immense benefit particularly in uncertain times since you will only ever pay for an item after a purchase has been made.

The entire business can be outsourced and automated after you get a hang of things. Customer service can be outsourced to several outsourcing companies or you could simply hire a virtual assistant or freelancer to do the job for you. A business manager can be hired from freelancing sites such as Fiverr or Upwork if you decide to completely automate the business and live off its passive income every month. But first let us go to the basics and fundamentals of the drop-shipping business. Let us learn how to walk before we attempt to fly.

This guide will focus on the following:

- The advantages of working in dropshipping
- Getting ideas on what products to choose
- Finding the right niche
- Find and work with the right suppliers
- Building the website
- How to run your dropshipping company
- The dropshipping model of business
- Shopify dropshipping
- How to dropship on amazon and eBay
- Taking a look at current trends
- Social media approach in dropshipping... AND MORE!!!

Introduction

Have you ever stopped to consider just how online shopping works? It may seem obvious to you, but when you buy a product online, there are generally four ways in which a seller can deliver this product to your doorstep.

They ship the product to you themselves. In this instance, the seller has the product on hand, packages it themselves, and ships it to your address. This is probably the most obvious method for sellers to utilize, but it necessarily the best for all entrepreneurs.

It is a digital product, and there's no shipping required. This is a wonderful situation for an entrepreneur attempting to make sales online, but unless you're in the digital publishing or software business, there's a good chance this won't apply to you.

The seller originally purchased the product, but has a third-party fulfillment service that ships their goods. This is a growing trend. As space limitations and time limitations make it difficult for small teams (or even sole proprietors) to handle a large amount of shipping and handling on top of their other business requirements, services like Fulfillment by Amazon handle the process of shipping goods as they are sold. The seller still buys the product, so the investment in terms of cost is actually higher than shipping on your own, but often the time freed allows for scaling the business and working on finding new products and working on marketing rather than the labor of getting a package to a customer.

The seller lists a product they have not bought, and a supplier ships the product to the consumer when a sale is made. This is known as drop-shipping, and the initial investment on the part of the seller is much less than traditional sales. However, with drop shipping comes additional costs for products and often additional fees, meaning lower profit margins per sale. However, because initial investment is mostly time, this means that more risks can be taken on a large range of products, and scaling the business can begin almost immediately, rather than when funds allow for it. This makes drop shipping one of the premier methods for those getting started.

While drop shipping isn't by any means the only way to reach a six-figure ecommerce goal, it is perhaps the least stressful and the most open ended. For this reason, many of us in the ecommerce field begin here even if we eventually branch out into other forms of sales as well. For those of us that prefer to put in the time rather than the cost, such as having a limited budget to start with, it is perhaps the best possible method of becoming a success ecommerce entrepreneur.

Dropshipping is becoming an increasingly common way to do business online, taking the fundamentals of ecommerce but simply adding a middleman to take care of the shipping and supply. There is huge potential to make an impressive income if you remain focused and determined while keeping on top of managing your business. While you may not be spending time packing and sending orders, there is still plenty of work to do, though you will be mainly focused with sales and marketing to grow and expand your operations.

Your customer does not see you. You are a ghost in the entire operation. Every step of this drop shipping process can be done with just a laptop and a Wifi connection. There is huge potential when it comes to this lucrative business model. Firstly, you do not have to stock any products nor pay for product storage. Secondly, you will only pay for the product after your customer has paid for it. You are using part of your customer's money to pay for the product. The remaining amount will be your profit of course. Hence there is zero capital risk involved in the entire operation. Talk about a risk free investment. However, like all businesses, your time and effort is required to make this a success.

The Entrepreneur Frame of Mind

The entrepreneur frame of mind is an important aspect of any business, and while drop shipping doesn't require the type of investments that many other business models would require, having the frame of mind of a risk-taking entrepreneur is still an important facet of being successful.

We may not display all of these traits, but a balanced entrepreneur does possess at least some of the following traits:

Willing to take risks. For us, this means a lot of time. We are able to avoid some of the financial risk, but any time spent trying to earn money is time spent not earning money from a more traditional route.

Smart about their risk taking. While the risk may be there, that doesn't mean we just jump into any risky opportunity. Running a successful ecommerce business isn't simply about throwing a fistful of darts and hoping one hits the bullseye. Sure, that's an apt analogy for the general process, but we are throwing these darts with an attempt at precision rather than throwing them haphazardly.

Looks for opportunities constantly. This is what truly sets apart an entrepreneur from simply being a small business owner. A small business owner can open a business because the subject matter is one of the things they love in life. An entrepreneur may be so lucky, but they are also going to be constantly looking for a new opportunity, a way to get ahead of the game, and a way to improve upon what is already available on the market. While we won't always be creating our own products, we still have to take the time to SELL these products. Being innovative in our approach is key to growing our business to earn us a six-figure income.

Isn't afraid of a changing market... which is great, because all markets are constantly changing in the world of ecommerce. There are always going to be new players, and the big players are going to be trying to keep abreast of things BEFORE and WHILE they are trending.

Motivated! This is perhaps one of the hardest things to accomplish as an aspiring entrepreneur. You need a REASON to want to become financially independent. For some, simply being rich is enough, but for many, we need to take the time to create a goal that goes with that fortune. Why do you want a lot of money? Why are you willing to work your butt off for it? If you don't have anything to work hard for, then why even bother?

Sees past the money. This may sound crazy, but the approach shouldn't ONLY be "what makes money?" What makes money today may not make money tomorrow, so if you operate solely on what is worth money, you can very often miss the bigger picture about why consumers spend the way they do. What does the consumer care about? How do we fit into their needs? And only then, how does that translate to earnings?

At the end of the day, the main thing about having the entrepreneur state of mind is truly the dedication to invest your time and energy. If you are prone to false starts, then it is important to realize that no great idea is going to take off until you change how you operate. For some, we only succeed in the "make or break" moments of our lives, but for your sake, I urge you to realize that working a steady job and getting paid a mediocre wage SHOULD be enough to realize that you're already in the "make or break" stage, even if you're not about to bottom out anytime soon so long as you stay employed.

Do you really want to continue making a mediocre wage and giving 5 out of 7 days of your life to someone else's riches? It may be easier to auto-pilot through a job you don't like, but I can almost guarantee you will be happier if you work harder and pave your own path. I'll end my rant here!

How Exactly Does Dropshipping Work?

Going back to the topic at hand, drop shipping is a fairly simple concept, and while the process may vary slightly depending on sales channels and the suppliers you are working with, the general steps are always the say:

A manufacturer makes the product.

A supplier (sometimes the manufacturer) offers the product for wholesale prices.

A business owner (or sole proprietor) lists these products for sale on their website or through a third-part marketplace like Amazon or eBay. They do not buy the product themselves for the intention of shipping it to the consumer.

A consumer purchases the product from the seller.

The seller (or a piece of software) informs the supplier that a product has been sold and either pays for the product immediately or pays for all sold products at the end of the month.

The supplier ships this product to the consumer on the seller's behalf.

The seller keeps the profit after the cost of the product, shipping, and any relevant fees.

The consumer receives their item, usually none the wiser that the seller never actually touched it themselves.

This is the simple explanation of how drop shipping works. Of course, there are many facets to each step along the way. For our purposes, we'll focus on working on listing products and working with suppliers. That may seem like two simple things, but the considerations are vast.

Is It Really Profitable?

The short answer is, "Definitely." The long answer is that like any risk, profit will vary depending on how well execution is handled, consumer response, and of course, the initial cost of products and any service fees from the supplier or third-party marketplaces.

It is important to note that while drop shipping isn't as profitable on per-unit sales as other methods, the sheer ability to list as many products as you want without upfront costs means that it can be scaled to tremendous size even as a one-man team. Have a few people working together, and the possibilities are pretty much endless.

Where Do I Start?

The best place to start is with some bits of knowledge concerning the investment that is involved in working on a drop shipping business. While the investment in terms of capital isn't necessarily high, there are still other forms of investment required from an aspiring entrepreneur.

Chapter 1 The Advantages of Working in Drop shipping

Limited Investments to Start

One of the best qualities of beginning an online store presence with Drop shipping capabilities is that there doesn't need to be a huge investment to begin. As long as the fees and enrollments are tended to the whole system can be a rather low budget costing. One must create a simple budget that is feasible in their situation and become more aware of the earning potential. The truth is that the less investment you put in at the beginning the less profit that you will get back in the long run or over time. This is not always the case if you can play good in the game of e-commerce. When the business first makes their step into e-commerce they also need to know their limits of investments.

It's important to get the basic steps in first before you jump all in with all of your money on one product shipment or filling the inventory to have every piece because we have to remember that the buyers are going to be an important part as well.

Remember that there is competition around every corner so consider the fact that there are other businesses like yours that may be in the same profit regime. We do not want to set the limits too low that they will not sustain the business model or standards set out. Just because there can be a lost cost of entry the truth is that you may need to invest more than the bare minimum to begin making the profit e-commerce will bring. Do not be intimidated by the competition that will be alongside your product line because there is room for everyone in this e-commerce world.

Easy to Get Started

This is going to be a small financial risk that you have to take and have to gear up for which moves we are going to make to see revenue come to our business. There have to be urgent actions done for the great experience of the customers. Information and product descriptions are going to be the next second habit that you develop so that you can also ensure that you are a master of your craft. If you don't know everything about the product line that's okay, but we recommend that you have some extended background knowledge about the products in your inventory just in case you run into a problem with a customer that needs extended information on the product that you sold and shipped them.

Lots of Products to Choose From

You may be considering the products plentiful to you and maybe adding more and more to your inventory as we speak. Do not stack this tower too high or things will topple and your inventory can come crashing down. Don't be caught off guard with too much to hold and a crashing halt. When the company adds too much inventory to their business catalog, there can be a difficult time moving inventory out of the warehouse and this can become problematic.

Some inventory may not be selling at all, and there may be other problems with popularity or bad review of products you have in your inventory. There can be inventory that you have that individuals have purchased and left bad reviews about on other e-commerce websites. This is a business that you can do in a global market and that means that you are going to expand your market through countries and cities everywhere. Do not judge any avenue that you try to market towards and reach out to every potential prospect that you possibly can find and define a better demographic of buyers.

You are going to find customers that are looking for a steady supply of the product line you have and there are going to be one–time buyers that will help your profit. Every customer must be treated the same with importance and respect to ensure that everyone knows that you are a reputable establishment. One of the basic things you are going to need at all times is WiFi and you will be able to track your online business anywhere you are at using a self-made calendar and an optimized application made for your money services. This will create an urgent mindset for the business because some order will come in and they will need to be handled with some time sensitivity.

Be aware that you will be supplying customers with products that they may rely on for their business. This is why it is important to follow these simple steps to create a useful presence on the internet. The business has to be profitable in every way for there to be an enjoyable workflow. Follow your instincts with product choice and get ready to begin. You are just going to get geared up for a few extra steps you must take you may not have heard of before. This is where we are going to be thankful we don't own a whole warehouse we have to both staff and management. We are skipping the middleman and we are going to become the go-to for our shop's great experience.

It's a Business That You Can Do in a Global Market

Global e-commerce is going to be a new world and you are going to find that you are not alone here. There are going to be striving companies just like yours that need the same amount of attention and passion to achieve the success it entails. Just because there are other drop-shippers out there with you on the web that doesn't mean there needs to be competition between two corporations. No business should ever have to compete with a business like Amazon because there is room for everyone and there is the same general focus shared.

Since it is a global market you are going to be taking orders and making shipments at different times and different places. You can practically make sales overnight and have your product in full rotation by the time you wake up to have coffee the next morning. There aren't going to be an open and closing signs for your shop because it's going to have a 24/7 presence online and this is going to maximize all opportunities for profit. Recognize that you may need to even do some interpreting because customers will come from every walk of life to just have one of the products on your line today.

We just need to figure out the best way we are going to market to our global crowd and how we are going to create a likable and shareable space for everyone coming to visit. Use simplicity when choosing your marketing points for your new global crowd. Our buyers must share the same interests and find the same importance in the business that is online. There must be deep connections and feelings attached to the store, and this is going to increase reputation value in more than just the community downtown. It is important to reach out to the customers that will build our foundation because they will spread our name to their close ones and corporations.

When we can establish a connecting and trustworthy space for your customers it's going to bring their close ones as well to the sites you set and this will create a greater fan base for your products. Once there is a strong structure of customer traffic you will begin to receive reviews to your store and the products inside and this is going to connect even more customers in the world. Others will be able to see new reviews that your faithful customers are kindly leaving and this is going to attract new crowds to purchase the other inventory they are unaware of.

This is going to be a new load of work since you are marketing everywhere around the world, but you are going to see a return come to your business because this isn't going to be a normal community reach. The global market you create may solve problems that customers have had for years as long as you can be a trustworthy source of supply and you will be the only shop that they choose to go to.

Easy to Scale Up

You may not be able to afford everything that you are going to learn about if you are starting with a low budget. But this is why we are going to ramp up production simply by just beginning. You will find more and more forward motivation with the decision you decide to make and that includes every shipment. Once you are making consistent sales every week and you notice that orders are coming in annually you may want to consider scaling up your productions. Truth is that you most likely are not going to see sales immediately come in the first day and especially if you have done no extra marketing for your site.

Give it some time and you are going to see a great return. If you have a high end and popular item in your e-commerce inventory, then we can consider the fact that you may need to get ready for the number of customers you are going to have right from the start to your site. Do not be afraid to use all means of advertising which can include user applications and social media to your advantage. Remember that you are going to scale up your store's traffic and that is going to mean finding a specific buyer crowd that has targeted interests. Look into blogs and forums that have other individuals asking frequent questions and give them helpful links to your store and see where it will get the business.

You are going to be an e-commerce shop that supplies the everyday individual and they couldn't need just a few units, but maybe a hundred units from your store. We are going to need to ramp up inventory capacity and find new ways to keep up with the demand of the customers that trust the businesses services. You may be selling a hundred or two hundred units a day and this will be because they are not high value enough to see a high return on. This will make your profits come in slower, but you will still profit nonetheless and we have to remember how much work this would be for one person every day if there were no warehouse with employees to make magic happen. Moving hundreds of units every day is going to take work and we have to be honest about this.

Easy to Automate

There are customers in other cities that will need your products on time advanced schedules and you can automate recurring shipments and this can give you so much time to do your other Drop shipping duties. Remember that there are tools that can do exactly what you have been asking for. We have to consider all of the ways that automating your services with other services is going to create a stable structure for learning about perfecting this craft.

Create templates that export sales orders using drop shipping systems. The inserted templates will then auto-populate when an order is received on whatever marketplaces or shop checkouts that the business deal with. It'll then be forwarded to your supplier as an email with a CSV attachment and this is going to act as an internal invoice. There will be agreements and surely; even a negotiated contractual agreements that assure the services provided will be fulfilled as well. Shortly after the order will be fulfilled, and all information that is about the product and package will be sent to the buyer for confirmation. This process can be done while the business owner is tending to other tasks unrelated without even having to opening an app or check in and out of tedious tasks.

VA's are a good way to go for a good way to manage your order fulfillment, and all you have to do is be one or you can hire one. Marketing agencies can handle your advertising presence online or in person, and there can even be a possible web developer hired and as well some electronic customer support system that you know the customers will be happy with in case running into any problem. Remember that you are going to be handling a lot in the beginning phases of the e-commerce shop so it may not be the easiest thing to dive completely into automated Dropshipping.

It is recommended that the business owner can get used to handling and shipping the products using every trial and error so that the process is all acquainted. We need to also understand that it's not necessary to automate your drop shipping system early so that you are trying to move out the entire inventory you have out the door in complete stress. The most cost efficient tactic the business can take for their online automation is critical, but we must make sure are all aware of the exact duties we must fulfill to run a successful online shop.

It is best to do the most you can with your e-commerce business on your own. You are going to learn a lot of dos and don'ts of your business and have full control of your business. There must be full control of the business so that you are not on the sidelines and unaware of any random occurrences. A dedicated owner is going to be at the front lines of their business and the customers are going to see it with trust. Your profit will be higher with a promise to expand even further with your global presence. Of course, this all only applies if you are in a growth/startup phase and you are at least somewhat able to do these tasks on your own.

Remember that you are going to be spending money on these services to automate the drop shipping done for your e-commerce store. Nothing is free, but there are some pretty decent rates as long as you find all of your options online before you make that choice with your trusted company. You are going to be spending money to do your business and it may seem like money is coming and in without balance, but it's your job to truly make sure that you are receiving pure profit if not breaking even to meet your monthly income plan.

Chapter 2 Getting Ideas on What Products to Choose

By now you should have a list of products that you would like to sell. If you haven't found a separate list of items that are trending, go through social media to find what people are talking about. You can also do a search online of the Top 10 Drop shipping Websites and check them out to see what they are featuring. You should always know what your competitors are doing anyway, from what they are selling, to what they are charging, and what they are not selling.

Check out social shopping sites, like Etsy and Pinterest, to see what is trending. You will quickly be able to see which products are getting the most attention. You will also be able to see what items are being shared and recommended.

Whenever you are checking out any products, some of the most invaluable information you can get is through the testimonials from those who have already paid and purchased these products. They can give you the pros and cons as well as alert you to potential shipping and customer service issues they experienced.

Wanelo.com is another excellent source of information. You can browse through a vast array of some of the best online stores from this single site. There are a number of different ecommerce businesses that are carrying a wide variety of products.

If you are a part of any specific groups, clubs, or support blogs online, check out to see what people are talking about. This, along with reviews and testimonials, will give you some of the most honest feedback on what people are loving and items that didn't live up to the hype.

Lastly, when in doubt, search it out. Enter a search for Top Dropshipping Products for 2019 and see what pops up on the list. You can do this for any specific products, for example, you can find out how successful skincare products would be in your Drop shipping business. After entering this search it showed that this category turned out to be one of the most profitable niches on ecommerce in 2018. Take advantage of all of the information you have at your fingertips through the Internet. All you have to do is enter a question you want to be answered and phrase it exactly as if you were asking a friend. You will be surprised to have the answer to your question returned to you in a matter of minutes.

Establishing Your Criteria for Product Selection

As you get closer to finding products you would like to sell, you should begin to set up the criteria that each product must adhere to in order to be selected.

1. Popularity. You should completely research a product to see if it is trending, and if it is, is it at the beginning or end of its run. Even if it is trending, it may not be worth it by the time you add it to your product line.

2. Price. What is the retail price for this item? Is it available as a wholesale item? What are my competitors selling the same item for? You may want to set up a section for low-priced items and higher priced products. Each group will attract a different clientele but it may let you know that it is easier to deal with higher-priced items than go for low-costing products.

3. Profit margin. Once you find a price for each product that you are comfortable with, you will have to adjust each one so that you can reach the amount you need to make the profit you set up for your business.

4. Repeat business. Is this a product that will automatically require repeat business? This could affect the price as it might make up for percentages if it made it up in ongoing volume. This could give you a small but regular income.

5. Target market. You must identify the type of people who will not only be interested in each product, but who will be willing to enter their credit card info so they can make a definite purchase. You wouldn't expect people who have a family that consists of small children to be interested in the same things as single millennials. Knowing your audience will definitely help you make more sales.

What are Restricted Brands?

When you are working through Amazon, they have a list of restricted brands that you are not allowed to sell on their site. Amazon restricts certain brands for several different reasons.

1. They are trying to keep counterfeit items from being sold on their site.
2. The company that has the products may already have exclusivity with Amazon.

3. The company may have exclusivity with an Amazon seller or sellers already

You will need approval to sell a restricted brand on Amazon. If you do get approval, it does not automatically mean you can sell all the items in a particular category. Counterfeit products are a very serious and expansive issue with Amazon. Instead of giving approval on certain restricted brands they make the sellers by these products directly from the manufacturer. You would have to be listed as a reseller who is authorized to do so. You wouldn't even be able to show or list these items on Amazon without prior approval. Some items may be okay to sell but only if they are in the used category. There are ways that you can deal with this situation more easily. It includes Retail Arbitrage.

What is Retail Arbitrage?

While the name sounds complicated, the process is very simple. Retail arbitrage is a process where a store, usually one that sells items at discounted prices, has items either in their store or on their website that you are able to buy at a very low price. You purchase the items at this deeply discounted price and resell it at a higher price and you will probably made a very good profit on the deal.

You may have read about a sharp businessman or two who got into the practice of physically going to stores like Walmart or Target and bought up as many sale or clearance items as they could and then resold the items online making enough of a profit that they were able to quit their regular full-time jobs.

Many times people wonder if the deal is so great, why don't the stores just sell the items themselves and make their own money back? The reason is these stores are so big with lots of inventory they often need the room and it is easier for them to just get the products out the door so they can bring in higher-priced items.

Retail arbitrage is allowed on Amazon but there are steps that must be in place. You probably wonder why potential customers don't just go into the stores themselves and buy the products as cheaply as you are. One of the reasons is that prices are not always the same at every major store across the country. A Walmart in Florida may not have those discounted items in one of their stores in Tennessee.

With the convenience of Amazon Prime offering 2-day, next day, and even same-day delivery, more people every day are shopping from the comfort of their homes.

If you are going forward with retail arbitrage it is recommended that you make sure you have the app for Amazon Seller on your phone or laptop. This will allow you to check to see if a product you are interested in selling is on the restricted list. Once you enter the name of the product you will be able to see if you can sell the item as well as what condition it has to be in for you to sell it – new or used.

There is an extension you have to have on your computer if you are looking for Items to resell online. When you open the AZIsight Chrome browser on your computer and you get to the product page on Amazon, you will be able to see right away if the item is restricted or not. This app is very comprehensive and will not only show you if the item is restricted, it will direct you right to a page where you can ask for permission to sell the item without even leaving the site.

Selling on Amazon will be a much smoother process if you go to the Seller Central screen and sign on to get the approval process started. You have to meet the requirements that Amazon has in place and be approved so you are able to sell products in specific categories.

Is Retail Arbitrage for You?

Retail Arbitrage is another way to make a decent amount of money through ecommerce. Instead of sourcing specific products, you are buying items that are deeply discounted as they appear in certain stores or online. You may have to physically go to the store that has the items so you can feature them on your site.

Amazon has been cited as being one of the best places to conduct retail arbitrage. The first thing you will have to do is sign up for a seller account on Amazon. You can sign up for an individual but may want to convert to an individual seller account. It will only take a few minutes to get signed up and once you do you will be able to utilize the free app that is available and will help you source your products.

The only app you need to start your retail arbitrage business is the Amazon Seller App. There is no charge for this app but it will give you valuable information. Once you are signed up you can scan barcodes with the camera you have on your cell phone. Once you do this you will be able to find out how much the item is selling for on Amazon and what the fees and costs are for each item you scan. This app will provide you will all the information you need to determine whether putting a specific item for sale will be worth it.

What you will need to know before you conduct the search is what the minimum amount is that you need to make on each item in order to make a profit. If the amount shown on the site is less than that amount you shouldn't even waste your time listing it. It is suggested that you aim for a return on investment (ROI) of more than 50 percent in order to become profitable.

When deciding on buying items for retail arbitrage, too much of a good thing isn't always a good thing. Keep your purchases of really good deals on the lower side. Depending on the item, things can change quickly online and you might make out okay on the first few sales but if prices drop unexpectedly you might lose money instead of make money.

Once you have your products purchased and ready to sell on Amazon you will want to enlist the Fulfillment by Amazon program. Once you send your products in bulk to them, they will, in turn, take care of sending all of the sold items to the corresponding customers. Fulfillment by Amazon has locations where they will store the items and ship them out to your customers as they are purchased. At the end of this book, you will find a list of the top stores to use for retail arbitrage using Amazon FBA.

Choosing Your Niche Category and Market

A common phrase that was used when choosing to embark on a career was to find your niche. In this case, it means a specific area that you feel comfortable in, have a passion for and are ready to make this area define you. If you love to cook, that is a broad category but if you love to cook Italian food, this would be your niche.

In the world of ecommerce, finding your niche category does have something to do with finding an area you are passionate about. When you are passionate about a subject you will naturally become knowledgeable in it and become something of an expert.

Finding your niche market is where you find a specific segment of a market, there is a problem that needs to be solved, and there is a large demand for the product but a slim supply. When you find something that fits these criteria, you will usually have an ecommerce item that could be a profitable item for your product line.

If you are serious about your Drop shipping business you have to put the time in to determine what your niche category is. This step will help to solidify your chances of success as you begin to sell items online.

So, how do you go about finding and defining your niche? There are several steps you can take to get a handle on your niche category so you can develop and expand your niche market.

10 Steps You Can Take to Choose Your Niche Category

- Make a list of all the things that you are most interested in.

The list could also contain any areas that you are most knowledgeable in. When you are interested in things and passionate about them your enthusiasm will be contagious and will draw customers to you who enjoy the same things. This would bring a receptive audience right to your site who would be primed and ready to buy the products you are excited about and are sharing with them.

This could start off as simply as how much you love your dog. If your dog is a specific breed he may have special needs or need or enjoy certain types of products that you could offer on your site. You may become recognized for being an authority on this type of dog and word of mouth, the best type of advertising, will bring you many new customers.

- Check out Amazon to see what the top-selling items are.

Keep an eye on Amazon because their information is updated every hour. If you pay attention and put the time in you just might be lucky enough to be in the right place at the right time,

- Open your eyes and your mind to everything you see.

Pay attention to what you see on television, what your friends are talking about, what the most popular items people seem to be buying, and what is trending on social media.

- Think of any problems that you think could be solved.

So many great ideas show up on shows like The Shark Tank. When we watch the people who appear on that show with a novel idea, we all wonder the same thing: "Why didn't I think of that?" Many of the ideas that do get the sharks to invest go on sale to the public a short time later.

- Don't overlook niche areas that will always be relevant.

When you are looking for just the right niche category for your niche market, there are a host of areas that will never go out of style that will always be able to provide you with products to source for your business.

These include:

- Weight loss items

Diet books – both old and new. There are many tried and true programs that are still relevant after years on the market.

- Exercise programs and equipment

These change regularly but things like yoga, walking, weight training, and running always have new information and most have the equipment required to get the best results.

- Cooking

This area has exploded and besides an entire network devoted to food, there are ethnic foods that never seem to lose their popularity as well as new trends that focus on getting dinner on the table in 15 minutes or less. Besides cookbooks, there are unlimited kitchen gadgets that pop up and people can't get enough of - a zoodler? A good set of pots and pans never goes out of style but there is always the gadget of the moment, such as The Instant Pot.

- Appearance and Personal Grooming

In 2018, cosmetics and skincare were some of the top sourced products on the ecommerce scene. Everyone always wants to look their best as well as stay looking as young as they can for as long as they can. Having beautiful hair, the whitest teeth, and the smoothest skin are always a priority for most people and there is never a lack of attention in this category.

- The Animal Kingdom

We love our pets. There is even an ad for a certain pet food whose motto is "Love them like family. Feed them like family." With that in mind, there is an abundance of products people will spend money on because they love their pets so much. They will plunk down their hard-earned money on everything from squeak toys to sweaters for their dogs to wear in the winter. And don't forget boots so their feet don't get cold.

- Family Life

Whether your child is 15 minutes old or 15 years old, there is no end to the things they need, want or just have to have. There are old standbys, like Legos and coloring books, and then there are new items, such as slime, the ever-popular video games, and of course, phones for the entire family always have to be up-to-date.

- Home is where the heart is.

Along with the ever-trending food shows, do-it-yourself projects and homes you buy so you can fix them up and sell them at a profit are the next best thing. There are Youtube videos for everything so it follows that after viewing a DIY project you will need the tools and items to bring that project to fruition.

- Look for items that have a price tag that is on the higher end.

If you take finding your niche market seriously and put the time in you will end up working smart instead of hard. Don't be afraid to go after items that are more expensive. You have a chance of making a higher profit margin with high-end products.

- **Clothing and Accessories**

Fashions may change every season but you don't have to go to Fashion Week to know what's in style. Check out as many clothing websites as you can, browse through fashion magazines, and just look around to see what people are wearing because that is what they are buying. Pay attention and make sure to jump on the latest trend as soon as you can because it could be over before you know it. Who would have thought that jeans that are torn up all over would be a fashion statement? Just make sure you don't act on anything that appears because you think you are going to make a fortune on it. Onesies and dresses for men have never taken off in the real world even though they keep trying.

Chapter 3 Finding the right niche

Niche research and product selection are among the most important steps in building a successful drop shipping business. There are no other ways around them. You have to do them if you want to increase your chances for achieving sustained profitability. I'm telling you right now that niche research takes time and effort. It can take you days or even weeks to zero in on products that you think will be embraced by customers. Niche research is about gathering data and gauging demand for your product ideas. In other words, it's a strategy for determining if it's worth it to pursue a product or not.

What is a Niche?

In the simplest of terms, a niche is a specific category or field in an industry. This is in business and marketing terms. For example, let's talk about the broad outdoor equipment industry. Under this industry are dozens of niches. The trail running community is a niche. The mountain climbing community is a niche. The cliff jumping community is a niche. The mountain biking community is yet another niche. And so on and so forth. Even these niches can be further broken down into even smaller niches. For example, the trail running community niche can be broken down into the marathoner's niche and the ultra-marathoner's niche.

Breaking down an industry into niches makes it a lot easier for aspiring entrepreneurs to find potential markets they can tap into. It allows you to look for niches that have less competition but have considerable demand. These are the two factors that you must always consider during niche research. One, the competition within the niche shouldn't be too tough in the sense that you can enter it and carve your own business in it. And two, there should be considerable demand for the products you want to offer in that niche. These two factors come hand in hand. Because what's the point of entering an uncompetitive niche if there's minimal demand for products. And what's the point of trying to fulfill a demand that's already being fulfilled by thousands of established entrepreneurs – profit margins will erode due to too much competition.

How to do Niche Research

Always remember that you have two main goals when performing niche research. One, you want to gauge demand for your product ideas. And two, you want to know the level of competition for those product ideas. You will be performing most of your research using various tools like keyword research tools and search volume trackers. Don't worry because most of these tools and resources are readily available and you can use most of them for free. Before you begin with your research, it's important that you already have an industry that you want to target. For example, you want to target the sports gear industry or the weight loss industry. I hope that you are getting my point here. The general industry serves as your starting point.

Create a Quick List of Your Product Ideas

The first thing you must do is write down a quick list of the products that you have in mind. Get a piece of paper and quickly jot down the ideas. This list will be your reference point when you start doing your research. Write down the words, phrases, and terms that come to your mind when you think about your potential products. Allow me to briefly illustrate what this list should look like. Let's say that you want to build a drop shipping business around the hiking niche. Furthermore, let's say that you want to sell hiking footwear on your drop shipping website. Brainstorming for product ideas, your initial list should look very similar to the following list:

- Hiking shoes

- Hiking sandals

- Mountain climbing shoes

- Hiking footwear

- Climbing sandals

- Durable climbing shoes

- Hiking slippers

- Tough hiking shoes

- Mountaineering shoes

- Mountaineering footwear

- Mountaineering sandals

This is just for illustration purposes. Your list can either be shorter or longer than the one above. It all depends on the products you have in mind and the niche that you want to target. My main point here is that you need to create a list of all your potential products. These should be the types of products that you plan on selling through your drop shipping website. Creating this list should take just a few minutes of your time. Some drop-shippers would even divide their lists into product categories and create lists within a list. Keep a copy of this list with you as you start with your niche research.

Google Is Your Best Friend

Google controls at least 60% of all online searches so it makes sense that the search giant has the most accurate search data and statistics. Needless to say, if you want to learn about a product's popularity online, Google is where you should go for information. Google has tools that you can use for your research. The two most important ones are *Google Trends* and the *Google Keyword Tool*. Don't worry, both of these tools are free to use. You don't have to pay a dime to gain access to their features and functions. For the Keyword Tool, all you need is a Google account. If you already have a Gmail account, you can start using the Keyword Tool by simply logging into your account.

For the Google Trends tool, you don't even need a Google account to access and use it. For best results, I suggest that you use the Chrome browser when you do your research on Google Trends. Certain features of the tool tend to not work properly when you use other browsers like Mozilla Firefox. Google Trends is a very powerful research tool in the sense that you can determine search volume over time, top and rising search terms, seasonality of search terms, and even the geographical concentrations of searches. You can identify which countries are searching the most for particular products. In the following sections, I'm going to show you how to use the two tools.

How to Use Google Trends for Niche Research

Here's a quick definition of Google Trends from Wikipedia: "It is a public web facility of Google based on Google Search that shows how often a particular search term is entered relative to the total search volume across different regions in the world, and in various languages." It's basically an analytics database of all searches on Google from 2004 to the present. Needless to say, Google Trends is a goldmine for data about ecommerce niches. It contains an immense amount of search data that you can collect and analyses to determine if there's interest or demand for the products that you have in mind.

Let's take a look at the tool's specific features:

☐   *Interest and Search Volume over Time* – This graphs searches based on the queries they received over time. You can quickly customize a time frame ranging from years to minutes. The graph will show you if the search volume for a particular search query is increasing or decreasing over time. It provides you with an idea if the trends will be in your favor or not. Let's say that you are planning to dropship trail running shoes. Google Trends will provide you with data if searches for the phrase "trail running shoes" is increasing or decreasing over time. If the trend shows that the number of people interested in trail running shoes is growing, then it's probably a good niche and that it's worth looking into. You can compare search data based on time periods. For example, you can compare search data this year to last year's search data. Or you can compare search data this month to last month's search data.

☐   *Interest by Region* – This feature enables you to pinpoint the geographical regions wherein your search term is most popular. It compares the origins of the searches. The interest data also reflects the popularity of the term in a certain region and on a certain time period. For example, you want to know more about the interest for "trail running shoes" during the first quarter of 2018. That's for the months of January, February, and March. What you do is customize the parameters in Google Trends so that it will reflect interest about "trail running shoes" during these months. The data will then show you the regions where queries for "trail running shoes" are most popular.

However, you should take note that the geographic regions are organized based on search proportions. Needless to say, some smaller countries might score much higher compared to larger countries. Interest for searches is scored by Google Trends from 0 to 100. You can determine search interest not just by country. You can further break down the interest data by states or provinces. For example, if you are doing research in the United States, you can access interest data by state.

☐　*Related Topics* – What this feature does is providing a quick list of other topics that the user also searched. Users searching for your term are also searching for these terms and topics. In our example, if you input "trail running shoes" into Google Trends, the related topics that you receive include the following topics: vapor, venture 6, sports shoes, tights, cross training, track spikes, back country running, vibram, under armor. This means that whoever is searching about trail running shoes are also interested in these general topics. How does this benefit you in your research for a niche? Well, it provides you with a ton of ideas about other products that your target market might be interested in. From our example, we can see that people searching for trail running shoes are also interested in running shorts and running spikes. These are products that you might also want to feature in your drop shipping store.

☐　*Related Queries* – A lot of people often confuse this with the Related Topics feature. The two are very different from each other. In Related Topics, you get a list of topics that the user also searched for. This means that these are general topics. In Related Queries, you are presented with a list of terms that the user also searched for. This means that people searching for your main term are also searching for these queries. In other words, these are specific queries. In our example on trial running shoes, the user also searched for the following queries: best trail running shoes 2018, black and yellow running shoes, file trail running shoes, brooks Cascadia, zero drop running shoes, best waterproof trail running shoes, Salomon speed cross 4, best trail running shoes women, and trail running shoes for hiking. These are very specific queries that the user is also searching for. Again, how will this information help you with your niche research? My answer is the same. The information helps you with more ideas about which products to promote and sell. It also provides you with ideas about other niches that you might want to further explore.

☐ *Top vs. Rising Queries* – When you look at the list of queries and topics under the Related Topics and Related Queries features, you can toggle the terms between Top and Rising. In Related Topics, the Top designation refers to the most popular topics. The Rising designation refers to topics with the largest increase in search frequency since the previous time period. In Related Queries, the Top designation refers to the most popular search queries. The Rising designation refers to search queries with the largest increase in search frequency since the previous time period. The data you gather from these features paint a picture of what's currently popular and what topics and terms have the potential to become popular.

☐ *Breakout Search Queries* – This is a feature which identifies whether a topic or a query is receiving a breakout number of searches. A topic or query is tagged as a "breakout" if there is a tremendous increase in interest and search volume for it. For example, if the search volume for "zero drop running shoes" last week was in the mere hundreds but during the current week the search volume ballooned to searches in the thousands. It will most likely be tagged as a "breakout" topic or query. However, you should be careful about breakout topics and queries because these are usually seasonal in nature. This is especially true for products that are seasonal. For example, Christmas sweaters are often tagged as breakout topics and queries weeks before Christmas day. For sure, it would be a good idea to start drop shipping Christmas sweaters but the interest will quickly die out within a month or so. If you want to build a sustainable drop shipping business that is profitable all year round, you should target products that are not seasonal in nature.

How to Download the Graphs and Data from Google Trends

On the top portion of each feature are buttons signifying actions you can take. Find the one that looks like an arrow pointing downwards. This is the universal symbol for "download". If you hover over it, it says "CSV". Just click on the button to commence downloading. Downloading will take just a few seconds. To open the file, just go to your desktop's "Downloads" folder. You can also embed the graphs from Google Trends. Just click on the Embed button and you will be provided with HTML code which you can just copy and paste into any page that supports HTML.

In a nutshell, Google Trends has almost everything you need to look for a profitable niche for your drop shipping business idea. For most experienced drop-shippers, Google Trends is all they need to find the next product they are going to sell. But if you are just a beginner, the data and information you collected from Google Trends may not be enough. That brings us to the Google Keyword Tool. If you are a complete newbie, I suggest that you make use of both tools in researching for your niche products.

Things to Look Out for When Selecting Products

Now that you have a good list of keywords related to the niche you want to enter, the next step is to zero in on the products that you are going to sell on your drop shipping website. There are several factors that you must consider, the most important of which are as follows:

1. *Price* – When drop shipping products, your prices should be competitive. It shouldn't be too high or too low. If it's too high, people will say it's overpriced. If it's too low, people will assume that your product is of low quality thus the low price. Most of the time, your customers are people who are too lazy to go out and

buy the product themselves from department stores or groceries. So it's okay to dropship products at a slightly higher price compared to department store prices. Most consumers will understand the difference in the price.

When you look at the price of a product, you have to consider the markup associated with the drop shipping model. For example, if a pair of shoes you are planning to sell costs $20 on a retailer's ecommerce store, you have to assume that if you are going to dropship the same product, it will have to cost a little bit more. The markup should not be too much in the sense that the gap between your price and the other retailer's price is too much for the customer to justify.

2. *Marketing potential* – The product should be an item that can be marketed online on most promotional platforms. You should be able to promote it via social media, blogs, forums, direct advertising, content marketing, advertising programs like AdSense, podcasts, etc. Your target customers are online and the only way to reach them is through online marketing channels. For this to work, the product has to be marketable on such a platform.

3. *Lots of related accessories* – As a drop-shipper, you have the option of selling accessories that are related to your main product. Accessories are a great source of additional sales and income. In fact, some drop-shippers make more money from their accessories than from their main products. The term

"accessory" is a rather broad term so allow me to explain it further in the context of the drop shipping business model. Let us go back to our example of drop shipping trail running shoes. Accessories that you can sell which are relevant to your main product may include the following:

- Trail running socks
- Shoe gaiters
- Shoe blinkers
- Shoe glue
- Anti-blister socks
- Five finger socks

Adding accessories to your ecommerce store is a great idea. They are usually a lot less expensive so they get bought much quicker. And not to mention the fact that they are easier to pack and ship. You can also try to sell accessories in bundles or packages. Use these packages to entice your target customers to purchase your main products.

4. *Low Return Rate* – It's far more strategic to deal with products that are simple in nature in order to minimize the chance of something going wrong e.g. one would expect to see a higher return rate when drop shipping a fragile ceramic plate which is more likely to break on transit, especially if it's packaged properly. Furthermore, electronic appliances are likely to malfunction which might lead customers to return them.

However, dealing with simple products like a shoe, T-shirt, tennis ball, phone leather/rubber case etc. isn't quite as risky. As a result, it's easier to meet customer expectations and you're less likely to get unsatisfied customers asking for a refund.

5. *Hard to find locally* – Look for products that are rarely sold in department stores and grocery stores in your area. This is a good strategy especially if you are planning to dropship products to a specific location. For example, if trail running shoes are difficult to find in your town or city, then it would be a good idea to set up a drop shipping business selling trail running shoes and targeting customers in your town or city.

A Quick Recap of Measuring Competition

As I have mentioned several times already, you need to gauge the competition for a product before you decide to add the item to your drop shipping business. The general consensus is that if the competition is very tough, you should abandon the idea and brainstorm for others. This is true in many levels but there is an exception. Don't abandon the idea entirely. The fact that the competition for the product is very tough means that there's a lot of money to be made with the product. What you should do is further break down the product idea into niches and finds the ones with less competition. This way, you are within a competitive niche but you are targeting a product with less competition niche-wise. Doing so basically allows you to take advantage of the demand while avoiding too much competition.

Another powerful way of gauging competition is by examining the number of organically listed sites on the first page of Google. Type in your main keyword and analyses the results. If several pages of the results contain the exact keyword, then it's a very competitive niche – these many people wouldn't be running ads if there weren't money to be made. Look at the top results and think if you can compete with them. Do you think you can optimize your drop shipping website and make it rank high in the results page? Or are the top results too established that it would be nearly impossible to reach or even topple them? You have to be realistic with your analysis especially if there are a lot of big brands in the top search results. For example, you are overconfident if you think that you can compete with the likes of Nike or Adidas when it comes to selling running shoes online. They have a lot of marketing power and a sizeable budget. You have to avoid competing against the big dogs by finding your own niche.

Find a Niche Where You Can Add Value to the Product

One way of getting ahead of the competition is to add value to the products you are dropshipping. This is especially true if you are selling a generic product (one that is also being sold by countless other drop-shippers). Differentiate your business by creating a unique value proposition. The next obvious question is how do you do this? One of the best ways to add value to a competitive product is to create a loyalty program for your customers. This is a great strategy if the product you are drop shipping has a high turnover rate. What you do is reward you're most loyal customers in the form of discounts and promos.

Another great way of adding value to a product is to offer discounts for bulk purchases. A good example of this is a buy one take one sales model. It provides customers with a nice incentive that is too hard to refuse. Your customers will be getting more of your products at fewer costs. For this sales model to work, you also need to negotiate with your supplier or manufacturer for lesser costs when it comes to bulk orders. You can also arrange to bundle complementary products your customers will like to buy together e.g. a tennis ball and a racket, shoe and socks of matching brands, phones and phone cases etc.

Another method of adding value to your product is to customize its design and packaging. Beautiful packaging creates additional perceived value in the eyes of your customers. When a customer looks at your product, the very first thing they see and feel is the quality of the packaging. Having a good product design could make the whole difference between a buyer and a non-buyer. Making the product packaging as attractive as possible helps in making the customer decide to purchase the item.

Chapter 4 Find and Work with the Right Suppliers

After you have chosen the products to sell you need to decide the source from where you can get them. You can make a list of the products and their sources using Air-Table or Google Sheets. This can serve as one database for future reference.

The supplier plays a vital role in the drop shipping model of business. He forms the crux of the entire enterprise. Therefore it is important to find a supplier who does his work properly and fulfills the orders in a punctual and efficient manner.

Choosing a supplier is the most critical step towards establishing a successful business. If a supplier messes up the orders you will be held responsible for it. Try to find a reliable vendor to supply your goods.

Criteria for Choosing a Supplier for Dropshipping

It is necessary to keep these points in mind while selecting a supplier:

Look for experienced drop ship suppliers who have cooperative sales representatives: Using the services of an experienced supplier is the best option because he will be familiar with the pitfalls and will be in a position to tackle them more efficiently. Along with this if he has obliging sales representatives who are willing to answer all the questions you will have an excellent team. This will have a positive impact on your enterprise.

Try to find a supplier who provides good quality products: If the quality of the products is good the customers will be more satisfied and less items will be returned. Your products will get good reviews and feedback from them. Testimonials will give a boost to your business. So it is imperative to supply products of high quality.

Request the suppliers to provide product samples so that you can test the quality before entering into a partnership with them. Ideally, the supplier must provide good quality images which you can put up in the listings of products.

Search for a supplier with technological abilities: While choosing a supplier ensure that he has the technological capacity to keep pace with the new changes. He should be able to grow along with the progress of your business. There should be no need to break a partnership with the supplier when you scale the enterprise.

Find a supplier who can do the shipping efficiently and punctually: If your supplier can ship the products within 24 to 48 hours you can ensure that your customers are happy. There is a lot of competition in the market. So if the shipping times are too long customers may not find your service very attractive.

It is a good idea to order some items from your prospective supplier and test how he fulfills the order so that you can take a well informed decision.

He should be able to communicate properly: Mostly the suppliers are in far off places or overseas. So communication is very important. The suppliers should comprehend the orders correctly and respond quickly. You must be absolutely sure about the capacity of a supplier to communicate properly before you choose one.

He should provide the facility to drop ship the items: All the suppliers of products do not offer the service of drop shipping the goods. Some of them are only manufacturers or wholesalers. So before contacting any of them, make sure that they do the work of dropshipping.

His fees should not be very high: Usually, the drop ship suppliers charge a minimum fee for this service. This is fair enough as they keep the stock for you and organize the packing and shipping part of the transaction. However, the fees should be around 2 or 5 dollars only. Do not select a supplier who charges more than this amount.

Offer fast shipping: Mostly the drop ship suppliers are stationed in China. It is not possible to expect instant shipping. But you can see to it that the goods are delivered as quickly as possible. See how much time they take to ship the goods to various countries. If it is between 1 to 2 weeks it is acceptable. In case, it is longer than this you may receive negative feedback from your customers.

Provide referrals: Good suppliers should be willing to allow you to connect to businesses to verify if their service is up to the mark or not. You should get a confirmation from other businessmen about their service.

How to Find Dropship Suppliers

You can use Google to search for suppliers. The search results show many e-commerce websites and startup incubators which contain complete directories and contact information of the suppliers. After you get the details of the suppliers who offer the products which you wish to sell, send short courteous emails to them asking some pertinent questions. This will help you to fathom how obliging their sales representatives are and know how swiftly they respond.

You may not know at the very outset whether a supplier is the right fit or not. But you can ask certain questions which will help you to make the screening procedure more efficient.

Screening Process
Here are a few questions that can be asked in the first email. Choose any 3 of them so that it is not very overwhelming for your prospective supplier.

- Are you ready to manufacture customized products if needed?

- Let me know your prices. Can they be negotiated?
- Do you charge anything extra other than direct costs? (Ensure that no hidden costs are there)
- Do you provide the facility to return goods? What is your return policy?
- Do you perform the functions of a retailer or direct seller as well?
- What is the profit margin that can be expected?
- Do the prices fluctuate at any time?
- Is there a guarantee or warranty offered for the products?
- Is there some dedicated representative at your end who will clear all my doubts?

- Do you possess and make use of one data feed?

These questions will show the supplier that you are going to take a well informed decision. So he will not try to cheat you or misuse the fact that you are a newbie. In drop shipping the relationship between a retailer and supplier exists for a long time so there is a need for some commitment.

Find Legitimate Suppliers

In order to avoid becoming a target of scams it is necessary to take these steps:

Make use of some online tools and check the domain's age: This will enable you to cross-check all the claims of the supplier with the facts. If the domain is very new it could be a scam. Besides this, if you check the age of the domain you will get to know the level of experience of the supplier online.

Check the reviews about that supplier online: In case, the supplier has cheated someone earlier the victim may have posted some warning message or a negative review about him. However, it is possible to manipulate the online reviews.

See if the supplier's business is registered or not: It is important to find out if the supplier's business is registered. You must confirm that the address given for his warehouse or office is listed as some commercial space or business place. If the search results show that it is a residential space it may not be a good indication.

Contact the particular manufacturer directly and cross-check the facts: You can contact the manufacturer if you are not 100% sure about him. But you should be careful because if the scam is a big one, the pseudo manufacturer may also be a part of it.

You can read various business blogs where the entrepreneurs discuss dropshipping. You can learn from their experience in this field.

Spot Fake Dropshipping Suppliers
There are a number of drop shipping scams which should be avoided. Watch out for the red flags and safeguard your enterprise from them. For example, if a supplier does not agree to take checks and accepts bank transfers only, it could be one warning sign.

A fraudulent supplier will not provide his address on the website or in his business correspondence. A legitimate supplier must display his address. Moreover, many scams involve a "membership fee." Though this practice might not be deceitful at all times, conducting a thorough research is highly recommended in such cases.

After you have asked the appropriate questions, taken due precautions and done the research you should be able to find the supplier who is the right fit for your business. With this you would have completed a major step in setting up your business. Next you can concentrate on establishing a system to run the daily operations smoothly.

Options for Paying the Dropship Suppliers

You can pay the supplier for the things ordered by the customer within 15 to 45 days. The products will be shipped immediately but you will pay for it later.

Otherwise you can chose the pre-pay option. That means you will pay the money soon after submitting the order.

Payment Methods
Credit card: This is the best way to pre-pay the money. The supplier deducts the amount from your card when the order is submitted.

Debit card: You can use one debit card to pre-pay the cost of the order. But there may be some suppliers who do not accept this method.

Dwolla: If a supplier does not accept either of the above cards you can use Dwolla. It is an online payment method for which you just have to pay a fee of $0.25.

PayPal: It can be used for paying the suppliers.

Directories for Finding Suppliers and Wholesalers

You can attend trade shows where you can connect with the major wholesalers and manufacturers belonging to a niche. It enables you to contact suppliers as well as research about the products in one place. This is useful after you have chosen your niche or product. If there is time as well as money at your disposal you can make use of such events to become familiar with the suppliers and manufacturers in the market.

A number of supplier directories are available online which are organized by product, market or niche. Many of them employ a screening process and ensure that genuine suppliers are listed. Mostly they are owned by companies who work for a profit and charge some fees for granting access to the directories. Some of them are Worldwide Brands, SaleHoo, Doba and Wholesale Central.

Frequently Asked Questions

1. Why is it important to find the right supplier?

Finding a suitable supplier happens to be one of the hardest tasks for e-commerce entrepreneurs. The supplier is your most important partner in the drop shipping business model. You have to rely on him for keeping your products in stock, for maintaining the quality of the items, and ensuring that the orders are delivered to the customers in time. A drop shipping business may be ruined in case a wrong choice is made regarding the supplier. So you should not make a decision in haste.

2. How to find a good dropship supplier?

Actually, there are two ways of finding good suppliers for dropshipping. You can manually search online or utilize some wholesale directory such as SaleHoo.

SEARCH ONLINE FOR SUPPLIERS: Type the name of your product and write "supplier" beside it in the Google search bar and see the results. Otherwise you may search on websites such as Aliexpress.com or Alibaba.com. A number of suppliers based in China use these sites for selling their goods.

Use some wholesale directory: You can save time and stay away from e-commerce fraud to a great extent by using a directory. There are more than 8 thousand suppliers who have been screened and verified on SaleHoo. You just need to click a few times and get into touch with some of the authentic suppliers.

Alibaba which is one online resource can be useful for finding and interacting with prospective manufacturers or suppliers. You have to ask questions and find out about their capacity to produce or supply goods and see whether they are appropriate for your enterprise or not.

3. Where can you find the dropship suppliers?

It is possible to find the drop shipping suppliers on shopping sites like Ali-Express, DH-Gate, DX and others. Moreover, they can be found on portals such as Worldwide Brands, DOBA, and Wholesale2B.

4. Where can you get the products for dropshipping?

Besides Ali-Express there are some other e-stores which provide items for selling. They are:

DH-Gate: All the items that are available on Ali-Express can be found here. The only difference is that they are more expensive. For instance, if the price of something is 9 dollars on Ali-Express it might be $11 here. So it is necessary to conduct some research prior to buying things from this site.

Deal-Extreme: its inventory is not very large. But it is suitable for electrical and mechanical goods.

Bang-Good: Instead of being one of the manufacturer's marketplaces it is only one e-commerce store. Therefore the cost of the items is high.

Tom-Top: It is a suitable site for tech items and contains around 1 lakh items.

Chapter 5 Building the website

The next step is to create a website.

Right, with drop shipping we can sell on eBay, Amazon or any other platform we want, but by creating our own website we have our own space within which to attract customers and make them part of our system.

Be clear, it is absolutely possible to create a profitable system without using a proprietary website. We can only sell on other platforms, save a lot of time on the development of the website that we can devote to expanding our catalog, or looking for cheaper suppliers, or any other business.

On the other hand, we lose control of the user experience, of what the customer sees and experiences during the purchase. In general, those who buy one of our products on eBay are not our customers, they are an eBay customer, and eBay will be able to enjoy additional information about this user as the possibility of advertising retargeting to sell similar products in the future.

It is an important decision that should not be underestimated. Finally, let us not forget the potential of these sales platforms (eBay, Amazon) as an advertising channel. You will have already received an item purchased on eBay, inside the box there was a ticket with a discount code for a second purchase, to be made however on the site of the seller.

This is an example of a very clever strategy that allows the company to enjoy the benefits of the eBay platform, but which drives customers to take their site.

My invitation is, therefore, not to necessarily create a website, but not to underestimate its importance, especially on a long-term activity.

Now, let's move on to the more practical aspects of creating a website. We can use many platforms that facilitate development work, based on our skills and the time we intend to dedicate.

One of these that I recommend is Shopify. For a monthly fee that starts at $29 and a percentage of sales (from 2%), Shopify allows us to create an ecommerce within a few days.

We then access to Shopify via the link www.shopify.com and proceed with registration.

The name

The first thing that will be required during registration is the name of the website.

This is a personal choice, but I recommend using an original and imaginative name, which evokes our niche but without being trivial.

For example, for a mountain bike accessory store, it could be a Bikey name, while I would avoid Mountain Bike Accessories because it does not transmit personalities.

One advantage is to have one of the key words in our industry within the name, for example "bike" is contained in "Bikey".

The domain

Along with the choice of the name, it is useful to keep an eye on the web domain. This is the address that will make our online store reachable, so it is essential to have a quality domain.

The domain must absolutely recall the name of our store: according to the example above, we could register www.bikey.com, www.bikey.it and many others.

Unfortunately, we have to deal with availability. In fact, not all the domains we will search for will be available. We can try to add other keywords, for example www.bikeyaccessories.com or www.bikeystore.com, or to change the top-level domain, for example to www.bikey.eu or www.bikey.net.

The possibilities are endless, and the result will be dictated by personal taste. However, I recommend, when possible, to buy a .com domain. If we want to work only in Europe a .eu can do well, and in Italy a .it, but we do not make the mistake of think backwards: if we buy a .it domain, we can sell all over Europe, but we will leave disadvantaged.

For the purchase of a domain, I recommend to directly use the panel of Shopify that allows you to buy it at affordable prices, around $10 / year.

There are providers that would allow us to save a few dollars a year on the domain, but it would be necessary to manually configure DNS entries, a technical issue that is not interesting for the purpose of this book.

Website design

The design of the website is definitely important. The web site graphics must be very clear and the interface simple to navigate.

A well-organized top or side menu is usually a good place to start. Using Shopify, we have available a variety of free themes that can be perfect to start without an investment and with a quality design.

Speech to be done separately for the logo. It can be simple or elaborate, monochromatic or in color, but it is extremely important to have a unique and recognizable logo. Those who are familiar with Photoshop or graphics programs can create it autonomously, otherwise you can get help from freelance designers, for example on Fiverr, starting at $5.

Payment methods

The site is ours, so ours is also the task to commit ourselves to receive payment. The methods are different and at the discretion of the entrepreneur. However, they are now universally accepted methods Pay-Pal and credit cards, through a gateway that can be Braintree or Stripe.

Payment methods such as bank transfer or postal order are optional: it is true that we could get a few more conversions, but managing this type of order is anything but automatic and risks taking too much time compared to the advantage we could expect.

On the other hand, the mark is to be avoided. Since the true sender of the shipment is not us but a third, there is no way to get the payment at the end of the cycle.

Online payments are sometimes subject to fraud, orders paid via stolen or cloned credit cards, fortunately Shopify and Stripe have sophisticated systems to report suspicious orders to us. Finally, in the case of payments with PayPal e-Check it is important to wait until the full amount of the purchase is credited to us before providing the order.

Shopify works well with PayPal and Stripe, which I recommend to use immediately for receiving payments.

Website trust

There are millions of websites, yet a good percentage of people trust only a few of them. Why? It is a problem of credibility, or professionality transmitted.

It is easy for a website to lose its credibility, so we proceed to points with a list of features that our website must necessarily possess in order to be seen as credible and transmit to the user the trust and all the information it needs to buy safely.

- *Service pages.* These can be frequently asked questions (FAQ), contact page, company history, information on payment methods, shipping methods and times, the origin of the objects or the quality of the manufacture.

All the pages that give extra information help to make the buyer understand that there is something else, that we are not just selling products, but that we are dedicated to every single product, that we care about the production chain and materials used. We carefully planned shipping methods to be used and expected the most frequent questions that might arise.

A contact page is absolutely mandatory.

With Shopify, I recommend the free *Help-Center* application for creating help pages and FAQs. Instead, as a contact page, it will be sufficient to use the standard template provided by Shopify.

- *Social pages.* Having a presence on Facebook, Instagram, Twitter is very important to make the buyer understand that he is not alone, that other people in the past have bought from us and found themselves well. We put links to our social profiles at the bottom of our website, and let's take care to have coordinated profile images to give consistency to the brand.

- *Social proof.* It is important to let users know the positive experiences of past buyers, as part of what is called social proof, or social confirmation. The reviews can be for the site in general or for the specific product, but we use the second option only when we have a substantial number of purchases: better not to have the opportunity to review, rather than having it with the item "zero reviews".

Still in the context of social proof, it is also useful to have followers on our pages in social networks. We therefore ask friends and acquaintances to follow us to help us in this adventure.

On Shopify, we can use a very ingenious system to transmit our social proof. An application called *FOMO* allows to show the user small notifications indicating the purchases made on the site in real time. This system, in addition to triggering in his mind the fear of losing the product (FOMO precisely, from Fear of Missing Out), confirms that other people are buying on our site, trusting us and believing in the quality of our products.

The *Ultimate Sales Boost* application has the same goal, but reaches it in a different way: it places a warning that indicates when a product is running out, or that a certain promotion is about to expire, or how many people are looking at the product in the same moment.

These strategies, halfway between social proof and fear of missing out, are extremely effective to push the customer to buy immediately - because postponing the purchase means that, in 90% of cases, this will never be concluded.

- *Trust badges.* These are important brands that our site can show to let the user know that the website is secure and recognized by other companies. We can rely on services like Trust Pilot, Norton Security, McAfee, but also design and apply the logos of our invention, such as an SSL logo or credit card logos accepted.

Of course, we use only logos and brands that have a real relationship with the website: if we do not have a score on Trust Pilot, we cannot put the corresponding badge, an SSL logo will always be valid because the website will use the HTTPS protocol for transactions, but despite being obvious, will give a feeling of security to the less experienced user.

Where to place them? We can have them at the bottom of the pages, in the footer, or near the description of the objects on the product pages.

In this regard, we can find many Shopify applications, including *Trust Seals & Badges.* I recommend trying more than one in order to find the design and positioning that most convinces us.

- *Press.* If we can publish our website, perhaps with a review of the products, on other blogs or magazines, why not take the opportunity to brag about it?

Let's write it clearly. Users who know these magazines will value their opinion and understand that they are facing a serious, professional and not improvised store.

The added value

The topic of added value has already been dealt with previously, and at this point it should already be clear to the reader how they intend to add value to the product sold through the website.

Added value and perceived value actually have the same meaning: this is because in the online purchase, the whole value of the object is purely perceived. Creating added value therefore means simply increasing the value perceived by the user, and this can be done with many different methods.

- Website, photography and high quality graphics. This is fundamental to the credibility of our website. I refer to the design we mentioned earlier, but also to the content of the website.

For example, it is essential to have photos of the product, since the buyer wants to see what he's buying. The photos should be of high quality, on a white background or on real usage scenarios, and if the object has a special packaging, it might help to show this in one of the photos.

Another aspect is the images that you see in the service pages, such as the home page and the company history: these photos must also be of high quality and not too standard, we can also take them on the internet, as long as the license allows us, but let's be original and do not take the same pictures that everyone else is already using!

If possible, we buy some of the items we want to sell. This will allow us to take real, professional or semi-professional photos — excellent photos can now be taken even with a good smartphone, if in ideal environmental conditions.

Finally, we can give these items to our friends and acquaintances to let us leave the first reviews on the website — reinforcing the social proof, as we have seen.

- The contents are very important. If we sell a product, we want its use to be clear. Together with the website, we open a blog dedicated to the sector of which we sell the products, or start a YouTube channel, or create a group on Facebook.

We want to create content that is really useful for fans of the sector, so as to become their point of reference not only for the purchase, but for their absolute hobby. Do we want to sell electronic components?

We can hope that someone will find us autonomously looking for a particular component, or we can write a guide to achieve something, that requires a component that we will sell. It's not hard to guess which method can attract more visitors!

First, I talked about blogs, YouTube and Facebook. This is because we want to show that the community is alive, exists and pulsates around our portal. To become a point of reference in the industry we must not provide one-way information, but be interactive and allow other people who share the same passions to know each other, to confront and help each other. If we can start a process of this kind, we will succeed in having a community that grows autonomously, and that will continue to follow our site and to buy our products. As the activity grows, it will be possible to collaborate with some of these people, asking them to write the articles for the website and, in fact, automating the creation of content!

-    Description and technical specifications must be comprehensive. In the creation of the products we are asked for a description. We do not try to dismiss it with a few trivial phrases. Rather, let's get involved and try to be as descriptive as possible. We do not forget information such as weight, dimensions or any type of technical specification can be interesting for the buyer.

So we create the website with images and descriptions of quality, some form of social proof, pages including FAQs, contacts and information on shipping. With the advice we have seen previously, we will be able to get a credible website and will have no problems in being reliable and attractive to customers.

If we use Shopify, we can get help from the many available apps, for example for badges or for connecting to social networks. Let's not forget, however, that the important thing is the result, that you get with Shopify or writing with code all the website, the buyer will see only the final website!

There is therefore no tutorial or specific way to realize our ecommerce. If it meets the basic rules we talked about above, it will be fine. Then we will see later how to get feedback from our customers and how to study their behavior to improve the interface of the site.

Chapter 6 How to Run Your Drop Shipping Company

You have already heard earlier about how you can start your business, but you have no idea about what you should do in order to run it. Studying about how to run your very own drop shipping company can save you some weeks and months of being frustrated.

Things Are Bound to Getting Messy - Since drop shipping is considered convenient, you can expect that it can be confusing as each sale can be complicated especially when other parties are involved. There will be botched orders at times. Some items will be out of stock. You may not be able to fulfil all of the duties you are required to do.

Keep it Simple - You already know that drop shipping is very complicated. You do not have to complicate it further by messing up your system. Make sure that you have created a flawless system that you will follow so that you can track down your inventory and the costs that you have to pay for every time. Instead of choosing some complicated methods, you can choose simpler methods that will do the job well.

Making Things Run Smoothly
The two things that are mentioned above are tips that will help keep you sane while running a drop shipping company. You have to be prepared to run things smoothly depending on the

situations that you will encounter. Here are just a few of the possible issues:

- *Your Supplier has Botched an Order*

Even if you already trust your supplier, there will be times when they will make mistakes and you now owning up to the mistake can make things worse. Here are just a few of the things that you can do:

☐ You may want to offer something else to the customer for free in order to make up for the error. It is the best way that you can smooth out the problem.

☐ Apologize to the customer for the mistake. If your customer is not aware that you have a drop shipper, it will only be confusing for the customer. Do not act like an amateur. Admit the mistake and do what you can to pacify the customer.

☐ Allow the supplier to pay for the mistake. Even though you have apologized to the customer for the mistake, it is still not your mistake. If you are dealing with a professional shipping company, they know that they have to pay for the error.

If the supplier where you normally get your items from botch up orders regularly, it is time to search for a new supplier. There are other suppliers who can offer better services than the one you are experiencing.

You have Trouble Managing Your Items

It is only common that you will have some issues with managing your items especially if you have not formulated the right system to follow. If you do a poor job, you may tell some customers that some of your items are available when they are actually out of stock. The constant mistake will turn a lot of customers off. You will lose a lot of customers in the process.

In order to manage your inventory, here are a few things that you can do:

1. Make sure that you have an application that will allow you to keep track of your items easily. We do not live in the Stone Age anymore. You now have a lot of options to make the management of your items easier. Make use of these applications and tools and keeping track of the various items from suppliers will be easier.

2. Have separate files for each supplier. It is only common that you are going to have more than one supplier in order to provide the different items that you need to sell. If you only have one supplier, then you will not have anything to sell if the supplier fails to submit the items you need.

Having more than one supplier can be complicated, though. You may keep track of all the items that you get from one supplier and separate that from the items you get from another supplier. This will allow you to check and see which items are truly out of stock and which ones you still have a lot of.

3. Do not just pick all of the products that suppliers are offering. It may be tempting to pick out all of the cute products that you see. It can also be easy just to choose products that seem to fit your business, but you also have to remember the quality of the items. Are the items worth purchasing? Will people actually pay a lot of money for the items that you are choosing? If you are unsure with which products of picking, choose primary items that are known to sell well.

4. It is okay to pick similar items from different suppliers as long as they look identical. This way, even if the items from one supplier run out, you will have a similar one ready that you can sell to your potential customers.

5. Always coordinate with your sales representative. Your sales representative is here for a reason, and that is to make sure that you will be getting items that will improve your company's name and branding. Always check if the items are available and inform your representative when to start purchasing again, so you will not run out of supplies.

In case even if you have tried your best to manage your stocks you still run out of certain items, tell your customer about it and offer another item that may appease your customer. If the item you are selling appeals to the customer, then you have nothing to worry about. It will even improve your relationship with the customer.

You Have Hired a Bad Vendor

A lot of the items that you are selling will be reliant on your vendor. When a vendor is bad, you will lose time in order to do other things because you will do nothing but follow up the orders of the customers and when they will be shipped. When you have a bad vendor, you can expect that your customers will be irate with you because they were not able to get their items on time. You may even lose customers in the process because they feel like you are wasting their time. At the same time, you know that by hiring the wrong vendor, you are wasting your time and money too.

Not all vendors are good so before you choose a vendor that will be your partner in your business, make sure that you will select a vendor who has already built up a good reputation. To make choosing vendors easier, you can base it on the following:

• *Have criteria that you would like to follow when searching for the right vendor. If one criterion are not achieved by the vendor, then search for another one that can fit your needs better.*

- *Make sure that you will set up a written document wherein your vendor will have to agree with the different terms and conditions that will allow your business to operate smoothly. The document that you are going to create with the help of the lawyer may outline shipping times, inventory updates, order exception resolution among others. This will let you and your vendor know what to do to have a good relationship and work together properly.*

- *If you have more than one vendor, create your very own vendor scorecard, so you will know at the end of the year who among the vendors you are going to keep and who the ones that you will part ways with are. You only need to do what is best for your business.*

When you have a bad vendor, you can cut ties with the vendor unless you have a contract that you have to follow. The moment that you are legally allowed to search for a new vendor do it for the improvement of your drop shipping business.

Dealing with Security and Issues on Fraud

Credit Card Information Storing

If you are going to host your own site, you have to be aware of the following:

- *Get to know the Payment Card Industry (PCI) rules. You have to be aware that this is going to cost a lot of money. There are a lot of compliance rules and audit that you have to be aware of.*

- *In case your client gets his/her account information hacked, it will be your responsibility.*

Knowing that it can be complicated, it is sometimes best if you are only starting your company, that you will not store the credit card information of your clients. You can start venturing into it once your business becomes bigger, but as of now, there are other options that are available that will not make handling your business more complicated than it already is.

Verification System

Since you are only starting out, it is okay to be intimidated with dealing orders and making sure that they are all correct. Remember that you need common sense and caution all the time.

Getting to Know the Address Verification System
In order to prevent fraud, using the Address Verification System will surely help. This requires customers to enter their address connected to their credit card in order to become approved. Through this, credit card thieves will be prevented from making purchases because most of them do not know where the listed addresses are of the credit cards they have stolen. It is already rare for fraud orders to pass through with this system.

It is evident that the order may be considered fraudulent when the billing address and the shipping address are different. If you do not allow items to be released when the billing address and the shipping address is different, however, you will lose sales if you would not allow this to occur so what the signs that you should watch out for in order to know if the order is fraudulent or not are?

- *The names are different - The names may be different because of two possible reasons. The first reason is that the order is fraudulent while the second reason is that the purchase is a gift.*
- *E-mail addresses do not seem authentic - It is very easy to create a free e-mail address but normally, people who use their e-mail address will incorporate a part of their name into it. If you see e-mail addresses that make no sense, this may be a sign of fraud.*
- *Most expensive shipping - Since a lot of fraudsters are paying with another person's credit card; they do not care if they pick the most expensive way to ship. Of course, this can also mean that they would like to get the items that they ordered immediately.*

So what should you do if you suspect that an order is a fraud? This is the time when you should make good use of your phone. Remember that since a lot of people would not like to put their real numbers on their order, you will either get a false number or you can get the number where you can talk to the person who ordered, so everything will be cleared. Honestly, this is easy to do in the beginning when you are not getting enough orders yet but can be more complicated and harder to monitor when you are handling a lot of orders at the same time.

Chargeback's

Do you understand what chargeback is? Basically, this is when a customer contacts his/her credit card company to complain about a charge that your company has made. The amount will temporarily be taken from your account, and you have to prove that you were able to provide the services or items to the customer who has complained of getting charged. It is okay if you can find proof but if you don't, there will be a processing fee charged to your account. The worst thing that can happen is you will not be given the privilege of having a merchant account anymore.

There are different reasons for getting chargebacks:

- Fraud

- *The customer forgot about ordering*
- *The customer did not like the item or service received.*

When you receive a chargeback, it is not the proper time to contemplate about what have gone wrong. You barely have time to do anything so make sure that you will do your best to answer as quickly as you can.

To Get Your Money Back

You have been charged a certain fee because of the chargeback, and your main goal is to get your money back. How are you going to do that? Remember to provide documentation which proves that you have delivered the items ordered from you. If the transaction is legitimate, your chances of getting your money back are certain.

To Win the Issue

You need the billing and the shipping address on the card information details to be the same. If the details are not the same, your chances of getting a charge back lessen.

Dealing with Returns

It may be easy to start making your own return policy without realizing how other suppliers do it. You have to understand the policy of each supplier that you have. It will make dealing with things easier. For example, they may have a 60 day return policy. When this occurs, you can be generous with your return policy as well. Of course, if you have more than one supplier, you have to consider all so even if there is one that offers 60 day return policy, if the other one only offers 45 day return policy, you need to adjust your terms.

How Customers Return Items

This is the process followed by customers whenever they need to return items:

1. A customer requests to return the item/s received.

2. You talk to your supplier about getting a Return Merchandise Authorization.

3. The customer mails the item back to the supplier and not to you. Take note of this. The RMA# should be specified.

4. The supplier refunds the amount.

5. You return the funds to your customer in full amount.

The process seems to be easy right? Yet, if you have tried returning an item that you do not like in the past, you know that there are different things that can complicate the return process.

Defective Items

When it comes to defective items, you are risking your business because people might not want to order from you again because you are selling something that does not work. Another bad thing about this is that you would have to pay for shipping. Unfortunately, you cannot pass on this fee to anyone else.

If the item is inexpensive, it may be a better option to let the customer keep the old item and just ship a new one, but if it is expensive, then you may have to ask the customer to return it while you handle the shipping fees.

Here are some of the advantages that can be received if the items are simply exchanged without the need for the defective items to be shipped back:

• *It is more cost effective - It may not be worth it to spend a lot of money on shipping the defective item back to you if the shipping is worth the actual cost of the item.*

- *You will score major points with the client - It is very rare that companies will allow clients not to return the old item anymore so if you do this, you can expect that your clients will be blown away and would be more trusting when it comes to dealing with you.*
- *You may talk your supplier into handling the shipping costs of the new items that will be sent to the client. This will depend on your relationship with your supplier, though.*

A lot of companies usually require the buyers to handle the shipping fee of returning various items that they have ordered, even if the item is defective. In order to stand out, you can order free shipping. You can expect that customers will take note of this.

A Few Possible Issues with Shipping Rates

When it comes to shipping rates, it can be very complicated if you have more than one supplier. Once again, you need to adjust your rates depending on the costs. To make the rates more uniform and less complicated, here are some ideas:

- *Type Rates - This means that you are going to have rates depending on the type of items that are being ordered by the client.*
- *Flat Rate - This may be the easiest one. There will be a standard flat rate that will be followed no matter what the items that are ordered are.*
- *Real Time Rates - You will have to compute the real amount of shipping based on the items that are ordered and the*

client's location. It can be complicated especially if the items that are ordered by the client comes from different warehouses. It is common for merchants sometimes to spend weeks contemplating on the rules that they have to make regarding shipping. One advice is this: implement a shipping policy that makes sense especially when the whole shipping expedition is considered. Since you are just starting out, take it slow. You will be formulating shipping policies that will make more sense in the future.

Shipping Internationally

Even though shipping internationally has changed drastically over the past years, it may still have some issues as compared to local shipping. If you want to ship internationally, here are just a few things that you have to consider:

- *Additional charges from suppliers because most of them will have different rates when processing international orders.*
- *Higher shipping fees that may result in some problematic orders.*
- *There will be excessive costs especially if you have to ship items that are heavy.*
- *There are different limitations that should be considered depending on the country that you are going to ship to.*

It will be up to you to decide if shipping internationally is actually worth it. It is not recommended when you are just starting out. You are always better off offering your business to local clients first. Who knows, probably in the future, you can offer to ship internationally.

Fulfilling the Order of Clients

It has already been discussed earlier that it is best to have more than one supplier as it allows you to ensure that all items will be in stock whenever people order but choosing the right suppliers that will help you run your company should be done with careful consideration. Some of the things that you should do are the following:

Choose suppliers based on location - It will still be easier if you would choose suppliers that will not have a hard time getting the products that you have ordered all the time. This means that if you have some customers that are within their route, you may choose them because of this reason alone.

Choose suppliers based on the items that they have available - You cannot force suppliers to have items in stock when they don't.

Choose suppliers based on price - It will be a nice idea if you can choose suppliers based on how they price their items but realistically, this is not possible because it will be complicated to figure out which supplier offers the best price.

Remember that as your business grows, the goal of suppliers is to give you the best items that you need. They will bid based on what your requirements are and usually, the one that bids the lowest will be chosen.

Picking the Carrier to Ship Items

The right carrier that can do the shipping for you will make a lot of difference with your business. Here are some carriers that you can consider:

1. US Postal Service - This may be the best carrier to choose if you are only shipping small items and if you are shipping internationally.

2. UPS/FedEx - They are well known for shipping large and heavy products locally, so you will not have any problems with hiring them for shipping large items.

Remember that when you are still creating options regarding your shipping, make sure that you will specify how long it will take before the products are sent. Choose the best choice for each order.

Chapter 7 The Dropshipping Model of Business

Drop shipping is an e-commerce model which involves online business. It came into vogue in the year 2006. The e-commerce stores of China were launched that year in the United States and Ali-Express got recognition. Few businessmen set up their own stores for making profits. They decided to use Ali-Express because it was less expensive for them. Other people also followed in their footsteps and drop shipping developed into a well-known form of business.

At present, it is one of the most rewarding forms of business which may be established with negligible or zero investment. Wayfair and Zappos are some well-known examples of enterprises which have adopted the drop shipping form of business.

New entrepreneurs, usually the Gen Zers and the Millennials use this model. They delegate the work of packing and shipping the goods to the suppliers this helps to decrease operational costs and gives them more time for marketing and customer acquisition.

What is a Dropshipping Business

Drop shipping is a form of enterprise in which you do not need to own an inventory, maintain a warehouse or store goods.

Moreover, you do not even have to ship the items to your customers.

A supply chain has to be managed in this model of business. The retailer does not own an inventory. He just focuses on promoting the goods and marketing his supplier's goods. In turn, he earns a decent profit.

As a drop-shipper the retailer acts as an intermediary between the buyers and suppliers. He receives an order from the customer and passes it on to the supplier. He keeps a certain amount of the money paid by the customer as a commission for himself. The supplier dispatches the items from his warehouse to a particular customer.

One new trend which is gaining popularity in this field of business is private label type of dropshipping. In this, the retailer requests the manufacturer to produce some customized items and dropship them on his behalf. Apparel with customized logos, simple keepsakes, custom made nutritional products, and pictures are some examples of such items.

How do You Make Money with Dropshipping
Actually, in this form of business, the goods are sold at a higher price by the drop-shipper to earn profits. For instance, he might sell an item for $300 or $350 while its wholesale price may be just $250. In this way, he can earn $50 or $100 as commission. He arbitrages the goods for profits.

Although the profit margins in this type of business are between 15-45% on a general basis, luxury goods, jewelry and durable items like electronics may yield 100% profit margins. **The key lies in selecting the right niche or product, finding the right supplier for the product, and entering a market that is not already saturated with that item.**

If you want to gain a higher profit margin you can use the services of the manufacturer for supplying the goods to the customer directly instead of relying on a vendor or supplier. Eliminating the middleman's role in the supply chain may improve the profit margin. But all the manufacturers do not provide drop shipping services.

In spite of some drawbacks once the drop shipping enterprise gets established and gains momentum it can become one money minting mechanism that does not need much input. Irwin Dominguez's drop shipping enterprise is a remarkable example of a business that earned USD 1 million in just eight months. It provides an affirmation for the fact that there is a lot of latent potential in this business.

Where do You Keep inventory

Drop shipping is a type of business in which the retailer carries on the business with no inventory. He buys things only after selling them; he does not store anything with him. The inventory is kept in the warehouses of the suppliers who fulfill the orders for the retailer. The stocks of goods are maintained by the suppliers.

The Unique Features of this Model

- The drop-shipper can set prices on his own.

- He can sell the products without partnering with some manufacturer. He can utilize platforms like eBay, Amazon or Ali-Express for this.

- The drop-shipper gains profits by arbitraging the products.

Gary V., Wine Library TV & Vayner Media Founder has rightly said, "There has never been a better time, in the history of time, than right now to start a business."

Chapter 8 Shopify Dropshipping

Shopify is a cloud-based and cloud-hosted online commercial platform which helps you manage and grow your business after you have started it. The best part is that you can start your business through Shopify from anywhere you want, provided you have a decent internet connection. Shopify lets you explore its facilities for a trial period of 14 days and later on, you need to have a subscription to get started with your business. There are three packages at three different price ranges that you can choose from depending upon the structure and size of your business. During your trial period, you can use the features of Shopify as much as you want without a credit card and at the same time make sales. You will notice Shopify allows you to manage inventory, products, and track your payments and shipping. In short, it is your manager and helps you to transition into the drop shipping industry. Also, accessing this platform does not require you to be proficient in design or be a developer yourself; you can easily teach yourself with help available online and by exploring its simple, user-friendly interface. As you can use Shopify from anywhere, you will find that you can use a variety of languages when sending emails, blogging, or dealing with checking out for the convenience of the customers. Currently, the available languages are English, Brazilian Portuguese, Danish, Dutch, Finnish, French, German, Hindi, Italian, Japanese, Korean, Malay, Norwegian, Simplified Chinese, Spanish, Swedish, Thai, and Traditional Chinese. Additionally, you need to have your domain set up according to your requirements and it is always advised to use a customized domain name. You should be ready to open a merchant account when you are setting up your store. After the customers have made their payments, the revenue is deposited in this account. Hence, you earn through this very account after you have fulfilled your shipping orders. You can easily accept online payments through third parties, who are known as payment providers. As drop shipping through Shopify lets you sell globally and locally, you can accept payments in multiple currencies. The types of currencies you have access to mainly depends on the third-party payment gateways or processors you have chosen to use. You are free to sell on multiple platforms that include social media, mobile, web, and online marketplaces. To start, you should simply see where this trial period takes you. All this information is widely available through various online resources thus, you should not worry at all!

How do you build a Shopify Dropshipping website?

Creating a Shopify account

This should be a very familiar step if you are comfortable with using the internet and social media. During this process, you will need a store name, so it is much better to have brainstormed ideas beforehand in order to have a catchy name. This name helps you set your store apart from your competitors and reflects on the products that you are looking to sell. You will need to register an account with Shopify and click the tab called "Get Started" - this is where you begin the process on their website. As you move along, you will get questions on this website so that they can compile information about your drop shipping history. Go ahead and fill them out. You will be given questions about your physical address followed by your email address. After you are done with these, the website will automatically take you to the backend of your store. Expect an official email from Shopify that has your store's URL in it. They will provide you with a URL in the email that will look like this: Your-Store-Name.myshopify.com/admin.

After the sign-up process, this is where the real work begins. You are introduced to the various features that Shopify offers and how can they be utilized for your store and business. You will be taken to your dashboard on Shopify and be provided with a lot of tasks, and based on your priorities and time you have, you can start working on them one by one. The most important ones are setting up your domain and designing and adding products to your store. Hence, it is suggested that you focus on these steps first.

Adding products to your store

Your store displays the products you want your customers to purchase, and your product line shows what your niche and vision is. If you have jotted down some ideas about what sort of products you want to have this could be an exciting way for you to get started. This part does not take that much time and hence, is most convenient for you to start with. You will notice that with just a few mouse clicks, you will be able to set up the items you want to display on your online storefront and seamlessly move the items around if needed. This helps in the long run when you are only focusing on designing your store. When you have an idea about the type of products your store will display, it is easier to build the themes and design the look. This saves you time and energy.

Oberlo is the default drop shipping application set by Shopify for entrepreneurs who are just starting their drop shipping business. In your account, when you go to the "Products" menu you will be able to locate the tab "Find more products to sell". This automatically lets you navigate through the Oberlo app. It is an application that helps you upload products directly to your Shopify store. You have access to a whole array of preset products in the app; you can find anything from toys to clothes within various prices ranges. It helps you learn your way around the app, lets you explore its library, and allows you to dropship the products directly on the doorstep of your customers. It doesn't get easier than this. Although you have to add products manually to your Shopify store, it is just a matter of a few mouse clicks. The application is user-friendly and allows you to import products directly from the Oberlo marketplace and Ali-Express. You do not need to worry about fulfilling your customers' orders nor do you have to think of going on a hunt for new or better suppliers. You can also write your own product descriptions, choose photos of the products, and much more. You will find their pricing of products on the app as well and can choose according to whatever your budget is. Overall, you have a manager through Oberlo that takes care of everything for you.

To add new products, you need to select "Products" which you should find on the left side of the screen, and then click "More actions" and "Find more products to sell" consecutively. The interface is very easy to use and you can use the search bar to look for items that you want to add to your store. Try to be specific and use the right keywords to get the best search results. You are free to add items which you prefer to your store by choosing "Select Product". You will see that there are certain costs mentioned on the product page. These include the pricing field where you are required to put your retail price along with shipping and supply costs. After all these steps, you should click "Add Product", and your Shopify store will have these items added by Oberlo. For each product, all you need to do is repeat these steps.

Editing details of the product
The products you are choosing for your store come with product descriptions with specific keywords. These words would be either similar or very different to what you were initially looking to use for your products. In cases like this, do not hesitate to make edits wherever necessary. This will require a bit of time and you need to put in the effort to ensure that the names and

descriptions of products displayed on your store are relevant and significant to the niche of your store. It is better to personalize these to make them more lucrative when the customers pay your store a visit. You need to have knowledge of what types of keywords work for what type of products. Apart from the right keywords, tags could be of great use as they can directly link to the collections and categories that your store is divided into. These labels help to make your store more efficient for searching and promotes ease of navigation for the customers.

Setting up a collection

According to your product line, you can further sub-categorize your products. You can do it according to your convenience or according to the market of your niche. Usually, you will notice that drop shipping stores set their collections up under various categories, which include items on sales, color and so on. This does not only help you to keep track of the order list and update the inventory but also makes things much more comfortable for your customers when they explore your product line. When you divide the types of items you offer under designated categories, searching becomes quicker and helps save customers time. It allows them ease of browsing and can be an important factor in turning them into returning customers.

To add or create a collection, you need to go to "Products" in the navigation on the left-hand side and click on "Collections". Then, click on "Create Collection" which will directly take you to a page where you can name your collection and add a description. The interesting part is that these collections do not have to be put in manually, they can easily be added automatically using filters too. Both types of collections can be used to your advantage but creating a manual collection is certainly more time consuming and contains only the products that you have chosen individually. With a manual collection, as you are working on this from scratch, until and unless you make an addition or remove a product, your line will display the products that you added. For smaller catalogs, putting this much effort in is worth it but for larger ones, this is not the most practical way. On the other hand, you can use filters and change settings when you create an automatic collection, which can help you create collections of items that are on sale, for example, but at a much faster rate than doing it manually, one by one.

Setting up your store

To set up your store, you need to click "Online Store" located on the sidebar on the left-hand side of the Shopify backend. Here you will be able to explore different themes, among which many of them are free Shopify themes. You can look into their theme marketplace as well and customize wherever necessary. You need to set up and design your store after you are done sorting through all the products. It is easier to transition into this step after you are aware of what you are offering as it helps you pick relevant themes accordingly.

If you want to customize and not settle for the themes already available on the site, you can choose the "Customize" option after you are done selecting a theme. You are allowed to make edits to the theme that represents your store's identity. There should be a toolbar on the left-hand side inside your theme builder. You can get started customizing according to your preferences from this step onwards. You can work with colors, social media, the checkout page, typography, and many other things when you are setting up your store. It is better to do trial runs when choosing a theme and play around with colors. When you have different versions, it becomes easier to make comparisons before making a final decision. Moreover, this customization also can also allow you to use images, which is the easiest way to connect with first time consumers.

Adding a variety of pages

Along with various types of themed content, Shopify also allows you to add pages about your business. Click the tab called "Pages" found on the left-hand side of the page and following this, you should click "Add Page". The variety of pages include an About page, a Contact page, Shipping & Returns and FAQ. The information on these pages makes it easy for customers to figure out any query they may have. Technical answers can be found on these pages and customers can find answers to their queries easily. It also gives customers a chance to look through the design and theme of your store. If you are comfortable with SEO (Search Engine Optimization), you can easily make modifications to the title, description, and URL in order to help specify what you would want your clients to see when they use the search engine to look for your store.

Setting up navigation

Navigating through a website helps you to understand the entire layout of the website along with explore various kinds of information on the website. The preset settings in navigation gives the customers the first impression of your store. These settings allow you to choose which pages or collections will appear on your 'Menu' tab according to your preferences. You need to specify and strategize how you would want your store to be perceived when clients pay a visit. You can put up an About page that allows your customers to quickly gain insight about your business and can attract them to your niche and vision. Many Shopify drop-shippers choose to upload their collections on their webpage to showcase the best of what the store has to offer. It completely depends on what you want your customer to see at first glance. Once you have that in mind, you can strategize accordingly. You should take time to decide which pages or collections you want to put up on the menu.

You should have already set up all of your collections, products, and pages before you begin making changes to your navigation. Now, you should go to the menu of your backend and on the left-hand side, you will find "Navigation" which lets you add any item you want. You will be able to add a link, a page, or even an entire collection. On the menu page, you need to click "Add menu item" and name your item. After you do this, you will see the "Link" tab where you can select any item that you find relevant from the entire list of collections, pages, and products that you have already set up. To add any particular category or collection, go on "Collections" and make a selection according to your preference. A similar method is followed if you want to add another page. If you want your menu to include the About page of your store, select "Pages" and then click the About page.

Editing the general preferences of the site

The title of your site along with the meta description can both be edited or completely changed depending on how you want it on the Shopify backend. If you are too hesitant to go out there and make choices, remember that there is always an option to make changes later on. You will find the "Preferences" tab on the left-hand side of the menu where you can make any changes you think would be necessary. Facebook Pixel and Google Analytics can be added to this section as well.

Setting up a domain

You may think that not having a custom name will not impact the performance of your business. To understand this from a technical perspective, it is possible for your store to work perfectly without having a custom URL, but you cannot deny the underlying benefits having a custom name will bring. Firstly, it gives your business a professional image and secondly, it attracts customers faster overall as it has the potential to give your store more visibility. If you do not consider adding a domain name, the default URL will be **https://YOUR-STORE-NAME.myshopify.com/** which is not easy to remember and read when you see it for the first time. You need to think from the customer's point of view and find ways that will help them understand your store's niche and appeal more clearly.

On the backend of Shopify, you will find the tab "Online Store" on the left-hand side. This is where you can find your domain, and connect, transfer, and buy a domain, whichever applies to your case. There are many domain providers such as Host-Gator and Blue-host, that help you obtain a domain. If you have an existing one, you can easily connect it with your Shopify. In a case where you do not have a domain through a third party, you can contact these providers. The prices for a custom domain have an estimated starting price of around 11 dollars for a yearly domain. If you have a domain already, the system can automatically link your domain name to your Shopify store. On the other hand, you are allowed to pay, manage, and renew your domain directly from the backend of Shopify. However, policies between your domain provider and Shopify may vary so it is much safer to have gone through both of their guidelines before making any calls.

Setting up payments

After you are done setting everything up, you need to understand how the payment system works. Just like the other steps, it is simple and easy to understand. You will find "Settings" on the menu on your left. Click "Payment Providers". You are allowed to make changes in the settings where you can state your preferred method of payment. There are some default settings which allow you to use Shopify Payments to make transactions. PayPal, on the other hand, contacts you through email after your first sale is made and gives you instructions on setting up a PayPal Merchant account. You should have sound knowledge in this area and choose secured payment methods to avoid mishandling and mismanagement.

Exploring other Shopify Drop shipping applications

The Shopify app store has a lot to offer and you should not settle before you have explored each of them briefly. As mentioned earlier, Oberlo is the default drop shipping app on Shopify but there are many others which you can subscribe to for dropshipping. Make sure you add ones that are relevant and most convenient for your product line. It is suggested that you compare these applications available on Shopify before getting a fully paid package.

Spread-App

The Spread App allows you to add hundreds of thousands of products to your store and gives you the flexibility to create customized product descriptions for your site. You can also display products from Amazon on your Shopify store. This means your customers can click on any product link and make a purchase directly from Amazon. It charges around five dollars per month, which is extremely affordable, even for a small business. Their services allow you to get automatic updates on pricing and inventory. It follows a very simple method where all you need to do is put the URL of the Amazon product on the Spread dashboard which then pulls the product using your Amazon API.

Selecting a paid a payment plan for your Shopify Dropshipping store

Investing in a good paid plan for your store is necessary for you to reap all the benefits of this user-friendly application. Of course, there is a plan available for free, which should be how you get familiar with Shopify but you should not rely on the trial version if you want to have long term growth. This trial period is 14 days; you should look into price packages according to your budget during these 2 weeks or well before them. You need to keep in mind that within the trial period, you will not be able to sell anything, hence, purchasing a paid monthly plan is mandatory to earn through Shopify. On the bottom of your dashboard, you will see "Select a Plan". All you need to fill in your credit card details after you have chosen a package and that's it! Now you can start earning!

Chapter 9 How to Dropship on Amazon and eBay

Dropshipping On Amazon

Dropshipping with Amazon is great and it is just another good service provider to sell products with. Selecting a service provider like Amazon will also include FBA and also FBA Fulfillment. When a Dropshipping company decides to go with Amazon for its product distribution it will open a few doors. First of all, Amazon handles all of the shipping and handling that goes into delivering the product. Amazon is going to pack and weigh all of the items and record all metrics into their system for data tracking.

The company will need to purchase electronic product storage space and also the time amount that they want the shop to be running on the internet. The space to sell will be paid for as long as the company keeps getting consistent sales with the product line. FBA will fulfill all of the needs that the customer has with FBA fulfillment. With this set in place, selling times and schedules can be optimized in many ways to handle recurring transactions and even personalized PO's from company to company. FBA fulfillment is going to keep track of all clients that buying on a routine basis by organizing their needs and the Drop shipping schedules that have been made to fulfill.

Amazon weighs the product per pound. These rates apply to any of the products shipped so there can be a good spending system at play for moving different varieties of the product value. As Amazon states, "Make sure the products are e-commerce ready."

This means that the company must make sure that the products they are going to be selling are practically already online and they are in a queue that is going to sell fast. One of the cool things is that Amazon will let you ship your products to them and the company can begin selling their company-branded items that are going to be great marketing for the company

Amazon also provides customer support for all of the customers and orders that are placed with the company. If there is anything that goes wrong with the package during shipment Amazon will contact both the buyer and the seller to keep full awareness of what is going on. This is a great play because most people know the name Amazon and they trust this name. It is important to stand with a trusted company if the company at hand has no name for itself. Although a few followers on the social accounts is great and shows effort it makes it all the much easier to dropship having a multimillion dollar company backing you up with professional labeling and a reputation that keep the company grounded.

Dropshipping on e-Bay

Drop shipping with eBay works the same way as with Amazon but there are different benefits like having bidding structures.

These selling techniques can welcome new sellers that have different product value and are looking for rare items. They use the same time of hosting platform. The business owner just purchases inventory space but there must be a good part on the seller if there is going to be a custom product sold. Drop-shippers communicate with many distributors and this is how they can supply such a diverse market.

Chapter 10 What to do next?

We know how to create a system that can capture visitors, turn them into customers and let them receive the product. And it is extraordinary to think that all this can work without our daily work:

- The customer comes from advertising campaigns, online research, marketing emails we designed.

- The order is made by the customer independently. Shopify makes it easy to purchase, PayPal and Stripe can receive money without manual intervention and get them directly to our account.

- The order is automatically forwarded to the supplier or warehouse.

- The package is prepared and sent directly to the customer who purchased it.

What's left to do? Optimize the process!

Every aspect described in this book can be deepened with dozens of other readings and dedicated courses.

We can therefore dedicate ourselves to improving advertising on Facebook and Google to reduce the cost of visits, improve the website to increase the conversion rate, work on email marketing to get repeat purchases and better feedback.

Once we reach a good level, we can *scale* the company. What does it mean?

Consider having a budget of $ 50 a day, which takes us on average 200 visits and 4 purchases. Since we do not have to worry about the infrastructure of the website, the shipments, the stock, what would happen if we double the advertising budget?

We could expect to receive double the visits, and then sell double the products.

In a real situation there are several variables, we could find that the cost per click increases if we increase the budget, thus allowing us to sell more but with a lower margin for each sale. On the contrary, the cost of the products could decrease with the increase of the volume of business, thanks to better agreements that we can get with the sellers.

A guide on how to scale business is beyond the scope of this book, but I would like to reflect on how drop shipping is a highly scalable system, because with increasing orders, our volume of work will not increase, but only the figures we will see on the screen — at the exit but also at the entrance!

The most important thing is to act, not be afraid to start a business, if well studied and planned, and especially if you are ready to learn what you need to bring it to success.

An ecommerce store structured with drop shipping can bring very interesting economic income, which can reach and even exceed a very high average salary.

All this does not come without effort: of course, we do not have to build a shop in cement and bricks, but we must learn to understand the functioning of every single component of our business, optimize, test and optimize again.

I hope this book may have given you an idea on how to start your business online using a completely automatic, flexible and without initial investment.

To improve, day after day, I still advise to deepen the topics such as web marketing, the development of ads on social media, the most effective email marketing techniques and the creation of sales funnel.

Chapter 11 Taking a Look at Current Trends

In case you are new to 2019, we need to talk about current trends and how they affect your business. You see, there are many different trends that gain popularity each year, which means they are booming in business. Knowing what these trends are and how they may work for you is a great way to push your drop shipping business to the stars.

Trends become popular and they are passed through word of mouth. Suddenly you're seeing ads for them everywhere and everyone is talking about it. An easy example could be the Pumpkin Spice Latte or avocado on toast. You don't know when it started, but these fads often already existed they are just in the spotlight.

If your niche fits you should be ready to capitalize on any current trends, and also be aware of them. This can truly make a difference in how well your business works. Just because you don't care about a trend doesn't mean it can't care for you; meaning, that doesn't mean you can't still make money off of it.

Knowing your consumers and understanding their needs is a great step toward creating a strong business model.

When trends emerge they usually do so suddenly, in an explosion that often takes everyone by surprise. That's part of the fun of following a trend. Of course, some of them are long-lasting and have been around for a while as well, so it's up to you to discern what to put your time and money into.

Now that consumers have more access to information through the internet and their smartphones, it's more important than ever to get on board with what they are interested in. This means that they can not only learn more about these things but then find and purchase them faster. Impulse buying is a huge part of sales these days.

Hopping on the bandwagon is a great way to lure people to your drop shipping business as well. If they see a product they've been hearing a lot about on their site it draws them to you. They could end up purchasing more from you, or using you as their go-to site if you treat them well. That's why it's important to have a smooth-running operation from start to finish.

Having access to this type of information means now more than ever you need to be active in your online role and pushing for those sales. It's so easy for consumers to find more about the products they desire or find places to order them cheaply. You want to be on their radar, and this means being informed about what they want.

Now that you have an idea about why trends are so important when it comes to your business and your marketability, we can go a bit more in-depth. Let's learn about a few of the trends that are relevant today and why they might be worth a second look.

Hopefully, you will find a few things that you can incorporate into your own business.

Current Consumer Online Purchase Trends Worth A Look:

Keeping yourself up to date on current consumer online purchase trends is a necessary part of your job if you want to find success with your drop shipping business. Picking up on a purchasing trend soon enough can increase your profits by a high margin.

Let's go in-depth and explore a few of those popular trends that are current moneymakers.

Health and Wellness

One of the biggest trends out there right now is health and wellness. This trend has been slowly percolating through the years, and now here we are, where it is one of the most thriving trends of 2019.

When we talk about health and wellness we mean more than just eating right and exercising. Wellness has expanded to mean so much more, including mental and spiritual wellness as well as physical. This can translate to eating more conscientiously, taking supplements, essential oils, meditation, yoga, and more.

The rise of fitness trackers has been picking up through the years as well, and people even track the foods they eat or the times they sleep, because now more than ever it is important to look after their health.

Consumers aren't looking to work too hard though, they easily jump to the next fad in the hopes it gives the results that they desire.

More than that, now consumers care about the ethics of the products they consume. So many brands have started preached cruelty-free products or ethically sourced material. This translates to a broader image of presenting complete transparency.

Health and wellness products involve more than just vitamins, they can also include organic products, smartwatches, and even the clothing that is worn.

Wanting to be "well" in all aspects of their lives leads to a desire to purchase a specific niche of items that fit into their ideals. This can include all basic products and beyond, so it's a great way to add it into your store if the desire strikes you.

As an example, going vegan has become ever more popular these days and is touted as being rejuvenating and a better option environmentally as well. There are also more and more products being manufactured that can be considered "green" and healthy for the environment, from how they are made to the resources used to create them.

Realizing that there is a whole customer base out there which cares about these things means there is a huge market available to create a business plan on.

Healthy eating is important and so is organic sourcing, but even the idea of "treating yourself" and working on taking care of your mental health has pushed all sorts of products out there. Bath bombs have taken off in recent years, and the more creative companies have made quite a tidy profit on selling them as a great treatment for self-care.

Self-care in itself is a huge industry as people flock more and more to the idea that it is important to take time to enjoy for themselves or even just look after their bodies more. That is where there are hundreds of thousands of products in this market targeted toward just that niche. Starting to get a few ideas?

Being a brand that is seen as progressive is a great way to build your audience and appeal to a wide range of people. Almost no one is going to sit around and say, "Oh no, they are environmentally conscious, I don't want to shop there."

When you're choosing the niche you hope to establish, you need to consider trends like this because there may be ways to fit it into what you are selling, or maybe it already naturally relates to it. Either way, be smart about it because health and wellness care aren't going away any time soon. People want to feel good and they want to feel good about themselves, and this is where that trend directs them.

Ethical Use of Artificial Intelligence (AI)
Looking at this section you are probably feeling a little confused, what does artifical Intelligence have to do with consumer trends? This is a big conversation starter these days is Artificial Intelligence grows more and more advanced and more and more businesses start using them.

AI and digital marketing now consistently work together, because it is honestly just easier to let the AI collect and analyze data. There are often common issues and ethical debates that arise when it comes to using Artificial Intelligence in regards to consumers.

Obviously utilizing AI can mean a better customer experience overall, because it can help curate content for that customer to keep them interested. The problem is, of course, when that Artificial Intelligence is considered to overstep the ethical bounds.

There was a whole newsworthy saga recently concerning the creator of Facebook and how their ads targeted, etc. Consumers are wary when it comes to AI because they believe their privacy is important, and it most definitely is.

Using AI doesn't need to be an ethical quandary as long as those who use it are transparent concerning it. AI can be of great use to any business especially when using it to amass and understand data.

What could be a long and arduous process for a person can take minutes and an algorithm for Artificial Intelligence? The issue is making sure it is used ethically, and the debate is about what those standards truly entail.

Utilizing AI is important, and so it making sure that they provide fair and unbiased results. Too easily it can be spotted that Artificial Intelligence is still taking up our natural inclinations toward bias. Amazon recently had to correct their hiring algorithm because it was unfair toward women. Insane that even AI has that issue, right?

Consumers don't mind brands using AI they just want to know that it is being used rightfully and ethically. If consumers don't believe that's happening then they consistently want the government to come to make a decision in regards to the businesses, which is a huge difference from when the tech boom began.

There are plenty of ways to check through your AIs or algorithms and make sure they are following suit with this consumer trend. It's your duty as the business owner and brand to make sure they comply with what your consumers desire. By doing so, and being transparent about it, you are opening doors for your customer base to feel a sense of trust and partnership with you that others might not.

Confused on how to go about this? Don't worry, IBM created a package that can help target any bias or issues within such algorithms, and you can use it to really in-depth examine the tools you use. Then you can start working on corrections.

Really, it's not too hard to be aware of the trends that are out there, especially this one, because you already are consuming products and are a part of platforms that are working diligently to eradicate problems in the ethics of AI usage.

So don't stress. It can feel like a lot when all these consumer trends seem targeted at holding businesses accountable, but now that you know what is important to your base you can start early. Use this knowledge to your advantage before you even open your doors to sales, and can't go wrong.

Legislative Brands

More and more consumers believe that businesses and brands need to be striving toward having a positive impact on the world and those they serve. This is not necessarily a bad thing, but its definitely making it a bit more complicated.

Going back to the idea of health and wellness, this is quite similar, as people push for ethical practices and consumerism.

Having a legislative brand means companies and businesses are using their power to push for legislation. That's right, our favorite brands want to promote their businesses by becoming a part of the changes that take place in our government and day to day life.

Imposing a positive impact is a great mindset, but there needs to be a lot of consideration when it comes to having those who thrive off of consumers money forcing legislation. Whose interests are being touted here? At least, that's how consumers used to feel when it came to this type of lobbying.

Now it is often expected for brands to push toward constructive changes that are better for everyone, at least, that's how it is being sold. The trend is for those who can make changes do so, and do good.

Instead of wanting companies to stay out of it, consumers expect brands to push for social changes and more. They want the brands to have commentary and dialogue concerning the politics of today, and that is a huge shift from just a few decades ago.

This type of branding for your company can be a positive and negative thing. Pushing for a plan that stands up to what you believe is right, or even just politically correct, can alienate you from a large customer base even as it collects you an audience. We see it all the time on social media and in the news because it is a huge conversation starter.

Choosing to implement a plan like this is something most brands think heavily about. It matters what your passions are, what your niche is, and if you can stand to be picky about who chooses your products. This is a trend that is more advisable for once your business is on its feet and you can afford to take chances.

An entire business model needs to be made in advance of this type of action, and unless that's your sole claim to fame there need to be serious safeguards in place.

It's more than just about appearing a certain way as well, you have to be ready to be authentic and listen to the voices of the people you are trying to speak for. This can be hard for many brands, and inauthenticity will ring hollow if you aren't following the so-called "rules" of the movements.

If this is a route that interests you, there do not need to be huge changes and promotions. Some things as simple as taking a stand on sexual harassment in the workplace, or providing more breaks and time off for your employees can show you care about what people are saying. Being a brand that cares can do wonders for your image, and also give you the chance to be a part of the changes that are being pushed for.

This trend is a positive one that you could choose to take part in easily. A few steps go a long way toward making a difference, and there's not really anything to dislike about becoming a legislative style brand, as long as you can handle any potential fallout.

Open-Source

At first, open-source can seem like a bit of a backfire. Putting out all your ideas and innovations out in the open so that anyone can take advantage of them? But that's all your hard work, isn't it? You worked on it and you deserve to reap the rewards.

Think of it this way though, now you personally have the opportunity to find ideas and solutions due to open-sourcing that you might now have been able to discover or afford to research on your own. The advantage here is that everyone can profit from this.

From an environmental standpoint, open-sourcing ideas is the best way to help everyone. Trying to blame big brands for all the issues out there just doesn't balance out when you realize that their contributions are still minimal in comparison to what is truly out there.

Here's a great example of a company really doing its part. A U.S. shoe brand called All birds created a unique product: a sustainable version of EVA foam. What that means is their foam is used making sugar cane, not nonrenewable fossil fuels. Not only that, they made the formula open-source so anyone can utilize this special foam when trying to create products.

See how open sourcing can be positive for everyone? Anyone who wants to create something using a foam now has an ethical option that doesn't do as much damage as other types. This is just one great example of how open sourcing can really help impact positively.

After a series of incidents at a Starbucks, the company closed the doors of its 8,000 stores for a full day to go through a whole new training concerning racial bias and how their employees should identify and handle it, that way there wouldn't be any more issues of that type. Once that was complete, they made their new training open-sourced so that any other companies could follow through as well, or utilize them when performing seminars of their own.

That was a great way for Starbucks to give back to their community and make things easier. There is no excuse to not have this type of training when the content for it is open-sourced and now readily available. See how this puts the pressure on other brands to follow through in positive ways?

Open-sourcing ideas and strategies is a great way for brands to give back to consumers, by proving they do care and they want to change with the times. What matters to consumers should matter to brands, and that's a trend consumers are easily swayed by.

Just remember that this idea itself isn't new or contemporary by any means. Open-sourcing content has been around forever, it's just now become more lucrative and expected for brands to use.

Take for example Volvo, who invented the three-point seatbelt in 1959. Hoping to help enhance the safety of the public, they made that patent open-sourced so anyone could access and utilize it, thus improving safety standards across the board for vehicles.

Coming up with innovative solutions and sharing them with the world is a great way to make a name for yourself as truly caring for the future and the productivity of others.

Not only can it help when it comes to bringing in an audience of consumers, it just makes you feel good too. The competitive advantages really outweigh any potential losses on this one.

Augmented Reality (Fantasy)
Escapism is nothing new. The art of storytelling is probably the most basic essence of humanity and goes back millions of years, to the art painted in prehistoric caves and even Egyptian murals and hieroglyphics. Before words, there were stories, and afterward, there will be stories still.

People want to believe in something more than them, they want to get lost in a world other than their own and feel immersed within it, and pretend they are someone else for a while. That's where books came from, and comics, and television, and movies. Now we have grown even more advanced as a society and have augmented reality.

Now that we have smartphones and infinite access to media, escapism continues to translate to longer and more interesting aspects. Adults can end up just scrolling on their phone for more than eight hours a day. It's not surprising there are more sophisticated methods to forget reality for a while.

Augmented reality is used by more than 80 million Americans every day. What is augmented reality, you ask? Well, in a simple answer, it is everything you already use. It's a reality that is superimposed into your hand in your phone or on your computer.

It's when there are real-world applications in a virtual space, such as using your phones GPs to get places, or when you play video games or watch television. Pokémon Go is a bit more of an advanced example of AR usage, but it utilizes your phones location system to track and place video game elements in the real world for you to play. You can even take pictures of Pokémon overlaid in real areas.

Another great example is that there is now a self-guided tour via an app for visitors at the Louvre. It involves integrating modern technology with real-world surroundings, and it is a fantastic development.

Something more simple just includes using your virtual world to improve upon the real world. Brothers John and Hank Green run many different businesses, and they created a non-profit called "The Foundation to Decrease World Suck". They marketed properly toward the younger age bracket, and they do 24 hour live streams in order to promoted donations to various charities. That's just one way they used their brands to influence real-world action and it is nothing short of incredible.

Your brand doesn't need to incorporate anything as drastic, these are just examples of how augmented reality is available in the day to day life and how it can affect the world. Many of the older generations often see this as a negative thing, but those in the market of business truly understand this is just another trend meant to improve quality of life.

Applying the appropriate types of escapism to your brand is a great way to connect to consumers, and attract new ones. Relating it to their real-life with as something as simple as a hashtag is a way to engage them that was never possible before.

Augmented reality is more than just the virtual experience, it's what the virtual experience can do for the real-world application, and the possibilities are endless. Find out what appeals to your niche, your audience, and you, and then see about incorporating it into your business model.

Chapter 12 Social Media Approach in Dropshipping

Social Media Marketing approach

A successful business does well marketing on public streets but the truth is since we are entering a new age of electronic future businesses must make haste for their change if they haven't gotten to it yet. This next change is to discover the new world of social media marketing. You are going to be reaching out online in many different ways. If there has been any previous advertisement experience had for the Business then one knows the power the word of mouth can bring.

Having social interactions with others build a great rapport with the individuals engaged. This kind of behavior is going to promote the global presence that the e-commerce shop has. Bringing in social media to an already online and trending topic is going to make with e-commerce a perfect pair. A business might have more than half of their following on a social media scale and thus in great odds will also make it easier to combine them into some good business marketing.

Bring the business to the front lines and where more than half the customers are; that's online. The web is going to be a strong motivator for content you are going to design your product line. Release a post about your new inventory and be descriptive when you tell the world that is going to pop and be a strong reminder to the visitors why they are going to visit your shop and ultimately why they will buy. Get started now and try making a social media account if you do not have one already.

There are tons of providers and many of them you will be able to market your business with. Create a login and finish editing the personal information on the account and everything that the business will be displaying to the public. Make the business account look nice and professional and it will attract business-like followers ready to see your catalog. Choose a provider that fits your needs or open two or many accounts to see which is going to work best for the business. The business owner may choose one social media outlet over another and this could give the business presence edge.

The only way to tell the right fit is to just jump right in and start designing. Social media has strong sources of the population that are willing to third-party market and this is why it's important to establish a bond with the community that surrounds. It can city-based or global to give back in many ways as long as you make the connection with your audience. Make their time worthwhile since they are spending so much online searching. Supply an online incentive that will encourage your audience to come back and share the content with other friends and family that are with them on these accounts. Find important partners that can also give you mentions and that will give you credible posts about the business you run and for many to see.

The question is can the e-commerce website survive from only social media marketing. This is not going to be a likely route because the only option the business has could lose it and have nothing left for support. If the company only dedicated their marketing budget to social media marketing, they are going to see the expensive cost burn through the budget quickly. Popularity is so important when it comes to running an efficiently visited shop but the company needs to take advantage of its capabilities to obtain followers from the social media sites that they could also be using, some of them even being free.

The more popularity you have the more profitable the business can be. The business can create very engaging motives towards their audience and they could attract more and more attention to the sites that are trickling into the shop daily. Keep gaining more followers and see what this popularity can do for the business.

Facebook Ads

Facebook ads are great and they are for any age range with a company structure. With Facebook as a company can market themselves from the bottom up and with little to no cost at all. Running Facebook ads can become costly if there is no following audience to broadcast to. If the company has no following on their web-sites then they are going to be paying money for company promotion and not for product promotion depending on how far we have gotten already.

These social ads are great because it engages thousands of people together for a common focus on the marketplace and this creates a strong playing field for posting products on any page. A company can pay for personalized ads that are going to air for the community to see sponsored posts on their pages and feeds so that they cleverly run into company products posted for great values. These advertisements cost the company upfront but they will also give great exposure to the presence of the shop.

The shop can post an ad about its new items or maybe marked down items that the company has extra inventory of. If the company can make an ad about the marked down items that are full in the inventory ware-house then products can be efficiently moved off of the warehouse shelves and into new revenue that is going to have the company break even with its assets. There has to be a balanced routine when it comes to paying for Facebook ads because not only can they get pricey but there will also be other ads that bring competition to the playing board.

It is in the best interest of the company to know exactly when to place an ad on the market. The company is going to need to be ready for any turnover and sales to skyrocket if necessary because if there is the right product niche the success is going to come pouring out. Customize ads with the company logo and titles that entice the customers to come on in and visit for the new sales. There is going to be opportunities to make a catalog or a flip advertisement and get creative with the cover flow when putting up an advertisement for the week.

Advertise on a good schedule so that none of the customers see the posts as spam and give the audience a chance to respond to the advertisement and give feedback about the current promotion. Utilize these ads when holidays come around and make an advertisement that speaks out above news in the Facebook place. This Facebook marketplace is going to create a level opportunity to see your posts and engage with the shop site that you like to involve in the posts. Ads can also be placed on the Facebook marketplace and this could include single items or bulk items.

This is a not usually the case because there are at times selling restrictions under certain sites but with Facebook ads this allows the company to list any variety of products. The company will be able to list products that can be sold as common goods or rare goods that are even handmade and at a limited source. Take advantage of the market diversity within Facebook because it will create a great opportunity to post and post again even when the product may not have sold the first week. If the product does not sell the first week through a Facebook ad markup the price and make the product bio look spiffier.

When the customers see that ad again they will have a new take on it and they will dedicate more time to considering visiting the shop site and picking out something that encouraged them to get there. With Facebook ads, it will be easier and easier for the average product supplier to have a global reach for the line in their shop. Global diversity is important so that every market genre can be tapped into and the company can take full advantage of selling their products to everyone around the world never missing a sale.

Google Adwords

With Google Adwords, there is going to be great diversity in search engines to bring plenty of crowds to the consumer website. With Google, Adwords google is going to place ads for the company on several landing servers and it is going to create ad space for all sites that are affected. Adwords is going to display ads for the company that relates to the company's mission or its makeup so that when someone is shopping or researching a site low and behold there will be an ad for the company and its product. This company ad is going to replace any space that may not have had an ad in the first place and this will create brand marketing for anyone who sees this ad.

Adwords control the ads that individuals see when they conduct searches like google searches for a specific product. This search is going to bring up many trending topics and depending on how much money the company decided to spend with AdWords the trending topic could the shop on a seasonal weekend. If the company is just starting Adwords is going to make a great opener for a company that has not built any brand advertisement. Lead a great advertising campaign by setting some money aside and spending it on advertisements every quarter to create a better-defined presence online.

This is going to maximize the reach the company makes on all of the audiences and this is going to ramp up production for any customers that have not seen or purchased from the shop yet. If product awareness can be brought to attention for the viewers all at once there could be a high spike of customers that come in to purchase all at once and this could send the company into a new stratosphere of sales. One of the main consistencies is the crowd flow and the amount of advertisement money spent which could be with Google Adwords.

Conclusion

Be prepared to take the skills that were learned in this book and transfer them into the next possible move in life which could be a Dropshipping business. You could be selling tee shirts or collectible seashells across the globe. Maybe your shop already has a company logo and now you want to do some brand marketing. Get aboard the Drop shipping train and enjoy the strategies you are going to learn through service providers like eBay.

Be aware that to run a great shopping website once you successfully take the plunge into creating a website for the company there is going to need to be security for every single piece of information that comes through the seller's website. Take care of these things with certificates that will encrypt your URL and links so that breaches will not try and attack the assets of your company and possibly even crash the whole site is complete and take everything.

Utilize marketing tools like Google Adwords and Facebook ads to gain full exposure to the community that you are engaging with. Remember that the comwunity is going to be an online base so there needs to be consistency if the members begin to become forgetful. Entice them with special offers and make every customer feel great when they come to your shop so that they know they are getting more out of it than any other shop they will trust.